Montage

Cinema Aesthetics

Series editors Des O'Rawe and Sam Rohdie

Since the 1970s, many academics and teachers have been taking the study of film out of Film Studies by producing curricula and critical literature hostile to notions of artistic endeavour and aesthetic value. An old heresy is a new orthodoxy, and the argument that the cinema exists solely to illustrate the politics of culture, identity and pleasure is no longer an argument; it is now a 'core doctrine' of film education, particularly in the UK and the US. The Cinema Aesthetics series aims to challenge this orthodoxy by publishing visually literate and intellectually creative studies that explore a specific term, critical category, or interdisciplinary issue.

Montage

Sam Rohdie

Manchester University Press

Manchester and New York

distributed exclusively in the USA by Palgrave

Published by Manchester University Press
Oxford Road, Manchester M13 9NR, UK
and Room 400, 175 Fifth Avenue, New York, NY 10010, USA
www.manchesteruniversitypress.co.uk

Distributed exclusively in the USA by
Palgrave, 175 Fifth Avenue, New York,
NY 10010, USA

Distributed exclusively in Canada by
UBC Press, University of British Columbia, 2029 West Mall,
Vancouver, BC, Canada V6T 1Z2

British Library Cataloguing-in-Publication Data
A catalogue record for this book is available from the British Library

Library of Congress Cataloging-in-Publication Data applied for

ISBN 0 7190 7038 4 *hardback*
EAN 978 0 7190 7038 9

ISBN 0 7190 7039 2 *paperback*
EAN 978 0 7190 7039 6

First published 2006

15 14 13 12 11 10 09 08 07 06   10 9 8 7 6 5 4 3 2 1

Typeset in Scala and Scala Sans display by
Koinonia, Manchester
Printed in Great Britain
by Bell & Bain Ltd, Glasgow

At the end of December 2004, I suffered a brain haemorrhage and underwent an emergency brain operation. I want to dedicate this book to the brain surgeon who performed that operation, Dr John A Jenkins, and to the doctors, nurses and staff of the Emergency Room, of the Operating Theatre and of the Intensive Care Neurological Unit of Florida Hospital (South) in Orlando, Florida.

Le monde te confie sa force en échange de ta confiance.
Pierre Reverdy

Contents

Preface

Before I began this book I wrote its preface, a before-writing that marked out an intention. The intention altered as I wrote. I realised that every entry was a beginning and the essential relation between each entry was not that of holding something in place in a carefully conceived, predetermined continuum, securing and mapping an order, but of relations of revision, transformation, circulation and returns. For that reason the writing of the entries was successive, the easier to alter everything.

Each entry refashioned those that came before even if nothing was actually done to them. Each had other places than those originally assigned to them since no place was ever constant; nevertheless, these first assignments of place have been retained. In any case, each is a beginning and the book a procession of beginnings, at the end of which, or at any point, the book begins.

Acknowledgements

I want to thank my wife, Lam Shuk Foon, Margaret, for her support, tenderness, toughness, love and good sense and my co-editor, Des O'Rawe, for his editorial help and encouragement and his friendship, warmth, passion, curiousity and wit over the years, most particularly following the haemorrhage and surgery. I am grateful to Peter Stambler for reading the book in manuscript and for his helpful comments and suggestions.

Introduction

The film strip is made of still frames that when projected at a set speed of twenty-four frames a second, give the illusion of movement and continuity. Film has had to reconcile these contrary directions of stillness and movement, continuity and rupture, and has done so in one manner or the other, most often in variations of the two. In practice, the different possibilities are considerable.

This book addresses what has always been posed by the cinema in this regard and always posed newly, historically and not.

Montage simply is the joining together of different elements of film in a variety of ways, between shots, within them, between sequences, within these. This book offers specific experiences of montage, not the application of a general model to specific films. For example, if continuity editing is shared by Ford and Hitchcock, their films are dissimilar and the continuities they achieve have unlike purposes. Equally, the discontinuites in Resnais and Godard are differently posed with different effects. These can be specified but are difficult to generalise or extrapolate and still be valuable.

It is particularities I want to highlight.

Though there are clusters of experiences and practices that films share in common, each film is specific to itself. This book is led by that specificity towards these clusters and away from them then back to the films once more.

This is not a work of theory that films might illustrate, but a critical appreciation in the form of essays, a reordering and an experiment, not a search for the definitive. It has no essential starting point nor clear end, no conclusions to arrive at. It is provisional, fallible, tentative, light-hearted.

Eadwaerd Muybridge

Eadwaerd Muybridge's studies of human and animal locomotion consisted of photographed plates that reproduced
bodies in movement in a sequence of still photographs he
published in 1887. These reproductions, though sequential,
were composed of intermittent, discontinuous immobile
units, in effect, a linked series of snapshots. Nothing moved,
no body, no animal, no stick, no ball, no hand nor eye, nothing went from here to there. The sensation of movement was
realised by the construction of a logical and progressive line
between one image and the next.

Movement was not seen, but imagined in the gaps between
instances of stillness.

Muybridge's locomotion studies though appearing to be
successive moments of a continuous movement were at
times faked. In these cases, he had his models pose in a
succession of gestures imitating rather than enacting movement. A Muybridge nude descending a staircase or washing
linen might, for example, hesitate at each step or each stage
of the process. It was her pose in suspension that Muybridge
photographed as if in movement.

Perhaps, except for scientific accuracy, it was not that
important if the reproduction of movement by Muybridge
was real or artificial, a matter of the camera capturing movement as it took place or a matter of hypothetical movements
staged. Muybridge was an illusionist not a scientist, and his

ends were commercial rather than educational. The succession of stills made the details of movement believable. Each shot was part of a consecutive series, therefore incomplete in itself, requiring a before and calling to an after.

Illusions so produced rested on a double disavowal. The gap between images needed to be disavowed (they were to be perceived as continuous) and the gap between the real and the representation of it equally disavowed (the representation appears as the reproduction of the real). The camera, in the details it exhibited, though it went beyond normal vision, only provided a more robust spectacle of it, since it was to normal vision reconstituted that Muybridge's photographs returned. Because the camera was a mechanical instrument, and thereby could be thought of as accurate because objective and non-interpretative, it guaranteed an identity between vision and reality. The camera was like the eye, but better.

It is the gaps between the still images and between the images and the real they represented that Muybridge's work 'covers' and in so doing produce an illusion of movement and of reality: not an analysis, but a spectacle.

In the pages of Muybridge's publications, the gap between one image and the next is perceptible, but in staging them into sequences, effectively editing the images, the gap is bridged by the reader (spectator), making a leap in time and space lured on by an apparent continuity and the wish, expectation or assumption of it without attending to its construction.

Muybridge's first photographs of the horse at gallop and the unconventional view his photographs gave of the horse's gait were first rejected as unpleasant. But this view was soon incorporated into what would be acceptable as accurate and correct. This in turn was integrated into a continuity of movement. The real that he had shown and that at first seemed unnatural in the end constituted only a minor disturbance in normal vision and conventional representations. The disturbance was quickly standardised, accepted as both real and true.

Muybridge first assumed a unity (the sequence he was to analyse), fragmented it into discrete fragments (the analysis), finally reconstituted it into a unified sequence again (reality restored). He was a narrator of subjects that moved, of characters in action. Helped by the objectivity of the camera, it seemed that his narration was less his than the consequence of his means, less an intervention than a recording, and by that fact (or illusion) Muybridge gained his fame.

Muybridge's images were not projected but printed in a book. Each page was a study of a particular movement or action, all the elements simultaneously present at a glance rather than consecutively as in a projected film strip, each effacing the other. The images of a series could be ordered in other ways, vertically, diagonally, and not simply along a horizontal. Muybridge would sometimes cheat accuracy to ensure the integrity of naturalness (the series) to overcome the inherent discontinuity of his images, the possibility that each might be part of another series telling a different story, unravelling the one.

Takeshi Kitano

> ... une image en mouvement, est évidemment instable,
> elle se décompose en beaucoup d'images (ne serait-ce
> que la multiplicité de ses photogrammes). Mais c'est
> sans doute le cas de toute images: toute images contient
> une infinité virtuelle d'images, et c'est l'un des jeux du
> cinéma, parfois, de faire 'sortir' ... **(Jean Mitry)**[1]

With the appearance of each hundredth number of *Cahiers du cinéma*, a noted filmmaker is invited to celebrate the anniversary with *Cahiers*. For n°600 (April 2005), *Cahiers* invited Takeshi Kitano. Kitano responded by proposing a game.

The game is based on sixty-nine photographs that Kitano took of various subjects at different times and places, mostly in Japan, some in Africa. The photographs, set out horizontally on two pages and numbered consecutively, are without apparent order, except numeric, and lack common themes. They can, however, roughly be categorised by subject. The subjects are banal, essentially disconnected, each oblivious of the other. There are portraits, mostly posed, like family snapshots: for example, couples in a restaurant side by side;

---

1 ... a moving image is obviously unstable, breaking up into many images (if only that of the multiplicity of the frames that compose it). But this is without question the situation inherent in all images: all images contain an infinity of virtual images, and this is sometimes one of the games (*jeux*) of the cinema, to 'release' (*de faire 'sortir'*) these ...

a young woman looking at herself in a mirror; a woman chatting with a bartender; an African in close-up making wry faces to the camera; two Western lecturers in front of a table. There are photographs of objects: for example, a Japanese sabre (*katana*) resting across the arms of a chair; a revolver; a porcelain statuette of a cat; a bas relief; a piano keyboard; an open book; a collection of magazines; a pair of shoes; a car; a motor scooter; a train carriage; its interior. There are photographs of events and actions: for example, a parade in Africa; the cultivation of a field; a boxer working out; a group playing music; a performance. There are photographs of sites, for example, a park; a bridge; a cityscape of Tokyo; Tokyo at night; a tomb; a train station; a construction area.

The game that Kitano suggested was to compose mini-narratives using any combination of four photographs from the archive of sixty-nine. Kitano made up fourteen narratives of four or five images arranged vertically on a page with captions by their side. The vertical organisation is not unlike painted Japanese paper rolls that began to appear in Japan in the eighth century (*emakimono*), pictures with stories set out in a vertical series, the story literally unravelling. *Cahiers* invited fourteen other filmmakers to create mini-narratives from Kitano's store of sixty-nine photographs, but whereas Kitano composed fourteen mini-narratives, the others were asked to compose only one each. This rule was not strictly adhered to and the result was sixteen.[2] The consequent thirty mini-narratives were published by *Cahiers* as a supplement to issue n°600 entitled *Ciné-Manga: La Règle du jeu*.

The mini-narratives are arbitrary and necessary: arbitrary, because there is no evident connection between the images in a given narrative; necessary, because once the images are grouped there appears to be a connection (causation,

2 The invited filmmakers were Olivier Assayas, Bertrand Bonello, Catherine Breillat, Arnaud des Pallières, Arnaud Desplechin, Jacques Doillon, Yervant Gianikian and Angela Ricci Lucchi, Hong Sang-Soo, Kiyoshi Kurosawa, Claude Lanzmann, Rithy Panh, Gus Van Sant, Apichatpong Weerasethakul.

linearity). While necessity seems arbitrary (accords are exterior to the images and imposed from outside rather than naturally motivated from within), arbitrariness appears as necessity (any image, though equally possible in the place of any other, is nevertheless, once selected, an exclusion of the others and conformable to a definite logic). The play of constraint and openness is unceasing, making every resolution irresolute and the definite uncertain.

While each image is a document (objective), the narratives are pure contrivance (subjective), real without being true, belonging at once to fact and to imagination. What gives the narratives their momentum is not linearity or causation but this double play, lucid, simple and very complex.

In the Renoir film, *La Règle du jeu*, guests are invited to a chateau in the country to take part in a rabbit hunt and later, on stage, a performance of brief amusements. The guests, like Kitano's photographs, pair off into various combinations. What begins as play and develops into farce becomes, in the end, deadly. The infantile theatrics of the guests in *La Règle du jeu* hide and bring to the surface secret and silent desires that only play can make appear, as with children's games of made-up rules.

There is a more profound echo of Renoir, however, in Kitano's game and in his films. Renoir accepts what is given to him on the set by actors, gestures, ambience and what is in his heart. Renoir's films are the consequence of encounters, inspirations, surprises that when met result in the joy and freshness of his works. It is a method of openness to chance, accident, error even, as if the films form themselves as they are taking place.

'*Ça la réalité!*'

The perfection of Renoir's cutting is not to cut out, to impose or to force a scene, but rather to attend to its natural conclusion. When it arrives, Renoir is there, receptive, curious, as Kitano is, I think, and ideally, as are their audiences.

Kitano's words arranged beside his images seem to follow rather than determine their vertical order. The words are secondary as with *Manga* where what you *see* is the story. In *Manga*, framing and scale are varied and abstract, the relation of images to each other rhythmic and melodic. Time is spatialised. It is something to see, hence the appropriateness of the first half of the title: *Ciné-Manga*.

If there are associations and echoes to other forms and instances (*La Règle du jeu*, *Manga*, *emakinomo*) in Kitano's game, there is also an element of digitalisation in it. The page of his sixty-nine images is not unlike a digital screen that presents a range of possible narratives and their combinations for editing and does so simultaneously, not, as was traditional in editing, successively (glue, tape, video transfers). There is no core narrative of images in the Kitano archive to be added to (expansion) or subtracted from (depletion), or even reordered, but instead, fragments of hypothetical narratives, potential, undefined, unfinished, crossing each other, folding, partitioning, tracing, touching, a universe of virtual, incomplete narratives that never cease occurring.

Digitalisation is not the condition for this game nor for other similar experiments in narrative and film (of Resnais, Marker and Godard, for example), but rather digitalisation is due to a shift in forms, perceptible some time ago (*La Règle du jeu*, *Citizen Kane*), to which it is a response and consequence, not cause.

A film image can find itself caught in a relation with other images in a narrative construction that holds it in place. But if that image is thought of as only passing through the film, as if on a voyage that provokes other voyages, with every position only temporary (Godard's *Histoire(s) du cinéma*), then, that image has other positions as well, other relations, not only a singular one, and that is the lesson too of Kitano's game. The act of disengaging an image from its context, whether real or fictional (all Kitano's images are so disengaged, precisely what allows their seemingly infinite re-engagements), is to disengage it from a world that has been completed that it might circulate towards other worlds not-yet, to touch down elsewhere, alight anywhere. Such decontextualisation is never a loss. Wherever an image has once been, it carries with it that trace in every new encounter, and so on, to other encounters (Resnais's *On connaît la chanson*, *Mon oncle d'Amérique*, *Hiroshima mon amour* and the films of Godard of course). The choice of four or five images from Kitano's sixty-nine for the thirty mini-narratives that *Cahiers* published and that are constructed into narratives do not exclude the images not chosen; to the contrary, all are present everywhere, made afresh each time.

Kitano's images are blank, opaque, silent, on the verge of disappearing to nowhere (*nulle part*), like the land of Nowhere that Jean Rouch enters across the river in *La Chasse au lion à l'arc*, where lions (one is called 'the American') are hunted with bows and arrows, ethnography plus *Red River*. Rouch crosses the river in search of a film that is document and story, fact and mystery, reality and imagination and that exists only on the other side, in the void of Nowhere, where a cosmos opens. Is not *Red River* a documentary of a cattle drive and *La Chasse au lion à l'arc* an ancient mythic fiction? It is to that void, to elsewhere, to other-than-here, that Kitano's photographs point, the kingdom of possibilities and imaginings.

Kitano's images, as in scenes from Renoir and in the best passages in Rossellini, are tense, taut, ready, attentive, erect, not contemplative. The images in *Viaggio in Italia* of the two lovers being uncovered in the ruins of Pompei at the moment of their death in 79 AD call to images in the present. They help unearth the buried sentiments of Alex and Katherine that had been compressed beneath the surface of things, unfixed, discordant, hence the ending in which they are reconciled, where the other possibility (not reconciled) haunts and makes inconclusive what is concluded, undermining it.

The secret power of Kitano's mini-narratives are in the opacity and immobility of his photographs like his rigid face, then the outburst, the sudden violence, the turning, that comes apparently from nowhere, from the other side, like a Rossellinian miracle, and that makes time rush backwards into the present. The force and energy of Kitano's images were opportunities for the filmmakers who had been invited by *Cahiers* to play Kitano's game.

In Kitano's film *Violent Cop*, the images are as if deframed, denied perspective, without borders or centre. In part this is due to Kitano's use of lengthy tracking shots whose direction and ends are not given in advance, and to the itinerary of the violent cop ('Beat' Takeshi, Kitano's other self) who comes upon things by chance or luck (the pursuit of the pimp and his deadly baseball bat into a labyrinth of alleys and blind streets where he disappears and appears, in a shadowy lure of hide-and-seek, exactly the same as Kitano's pursuit of the sadistic killer drug dealer). The camera follows Kitano's uncertain, silent, determined itineraries and the explosions that erupt as he proceeds. Anything can happen. Every image, however plain or banal, is charged with that possibility and points, like his sixty-nine *ciné-manga* images in multiple directions each beyond itself. Because there is no centre or perspective (exacerbated by Kitano's tracks and overhead shots), the image spills over its frame, emphasising a surface (an expanse) not a depth (interior).

The impassivity of 'Beat' Takeshi and the opacity of his motives make him a purely physical figure, of gestures, fists, agonies, looks, gaits (bow-legged), and sounds (a monosyllabic, guttural mumbling) without psychological depth or dramatic interiority. He becomes the image, is its movement, rhythm, beat, tics, flashes of illumination.

Violent Cop is an action film where story is subordinate to elements as fleeting as bodies in motion and where characters are defined, as in a Hawks film, by what they do, how they appear, and the way they regard, not what they say. And this is the film. It runs beneath or beside the story as the sixty-nine images by the side of the narratives.

When Dude in *Rio Bravo* crawls on the ground to pick out the silver dollar that Burdett had tauntingly thrown into a spitoon at the very beginning of the film, it is as if the movement forward of the story hesitates for an instant at his gesture, intensifying it and the slime of the dollar in the spitoon, then resumes its path taking Dude's movement, his face, his look, his clothes along with it yet the gesture remains as a residue. Such residues are the film, highlighted by an editing ('classic') that serves not simply the narrative function often assigned to it of continuation.

What connects the sixty-nine images of Kitano's *Ciné-Manga: La Règle du jeu* is the emptiness they evoke and that surrounds and conditions them, an emptiness directly related to their virtual possibilities and the multiplicities they suggest. It is not the false fullness of consequence found in Muybridge or a contemporary cinema whose images always have somewhere definite to go. It is instead the true fullness of going nowhere in particular.

Takeshi Kitano (2)

Each one of Kitano's sixty-nine images contains a narrative and each of the thirty mini-narratives composed by him and by other filmmakers using the archive of sixty-nine images begins with an image, not a narrative or a script. The images do not illustrate a written text, nor do they follow any pre-arranged, pre-existing pattern.

The 'classical' film, above all, belonged to a system of legibility. What you see in the film must make sense. The images above all serve that legibility. If you think of a film by Hawks, for example, it is not what you see that is important but what you understand of what you see. For Hawks, lucidity is not a function of the visual, but rather the reverse; the visual is a means to serve the ends of lucidity.

Kitano's game, and his films, proceed from different assumptions. In his game, the images illustrate nothing. They are open, and, because of their openness, illegible and ambiguous (except as tautologies where each image is a representation of what it represents). You begin with one image and it suggests another one by all manner of associations, but primarily visual ones. In the usual course of a montage of images, certainly one of linearity, the 'next' image is a modifier of the previous image but in a strict line of continuity so that what you understand is causation and consequence.

The modifications caused by a succession of images in the

Kitano game, limited to three, four or five images at most, create a radical modification of all of them as the images are joined, but of a different order than the 'classical' modification since each Kitano image (not immediately legible) is a means to penetrate and reveal the other images, not as a succession of events, but as a study of images. If the first image chosen is altered by succeeding ones, none is what they were to begin with. Each image is more than it appears to be and is certainly not, as is crucial in a 'classical' system, univocal and unified. Effectively, Kitano's narratives, rather than placing limits on his images, shatter any singularity that might be supposed for them. To see any Kitano image is to see it again (that is part of his system) and seeing it again is to see it differently and to see it as a possibility. In a film by Hawks, you begin with an idea: definite, clear, logical. In Kitano's game and in his films, it is important, to begin with nothing.

What was radical in Bazin's position about montage was not his objection to montage as such (which would have been, if true, absurd), but a position in favour of the openness of images as opposed to images pre-digested and signified in advance as in a cinema dominated by the script and by its organisation of images (*découpage*). As Godard has exemplified in his films and in his early writings on montage and classical construction, montage can function just as well, if not better, than a sequence-shot or depth-of-field shot or the moving camera or lens, to open an image up, to disturb any univocal understanding of it, to shatter its unity, to make ambiguous and to reveal the multiplicities and variety of directions contained in every image, in short to unfix images and films. Making a film in this way (and watching one) is an adventure in regarding and seeing again, each time for the first time and with little else to go on than the strength of the images that force you to see and thereby liberate your imagination. Bazin and the *Nouvelle Vague* directors and critics who were inspired by him, like Godard, helped to give birth to a new cinema and one that Kitano has inherited.

It is perfectly fitting that Kitano was honoured by *Cahiers du cinéma* and that he invited *Cahiers* to play a game that was already theirs.

Pier Paolo Pasolini

... toute grande oeuvre est un genre à elle toute seule et exige d'être comprise en tant que tal ...

Le pire advient lorsque les débats sur la théorie et la méthode remplaçant la connaissance des oeuvres, et avec, l'illusion qu'une méthode consiste en 'des règles qu'on pourrait appliquer' ... Ces considérations prétendent établir des certitudes là ou l'oeuvre d'art est essentiellement incertaine. **(Youssef Ishaghpour)** [3]

Pasolini's film theory is a sustained opposition to what he called naturalism, a phenomenon that he principally identified with Italian neo-realism. His theory was based on, in his own words, a heretical understanding of semiotics. The construction of the theory relied entirely on the use of analogies. The semiotic heresy was his positing of reality as language, as already and primarily linguistic, as in the analogy reality is like a language.

Pasolini asserted that reality was what Saussure called language or *langue* whose units for articulation were nothing

---

3 ... every great work is a genre in itself standing alone and it must be understood in that way ...

The worst is when debates on theory and method replace an understanding of the works and under the illusion that a method consists of 'rules that can be applied' ... Such views pretend to establish certitudes whereas the work of art is essentially uncertain.

less than reality itself. The cinema, he said, duplicated reality and thus while reality was a *langue*, cinema could be thought of as the written language of reality insofar as it depended on it to create its filmic images (duplications of the real). In short, the cinema wrote with reality. Cinema so conceived was caught within a two-fold analogy: it was like language and like reality, and these analogies related to another, namely, that reality was like a language. Cinema was a virtual system actualised in films in the same way that *langue* was actualised in the concrete utterances of speech, of *paroles*. In a spiralling chain of analogies reality was made to be like a language and cinema like the language of reality, though written, and films like the speech of that language that depend on cinema for its units of articulation. His theory is a complex system of associative analogical relations, metaphorical chains, less analytic than poetic.

Significance and sense were to be found only in specific films (*paroles*) and not in the system of cinema which had neither finitude nor boundaries. In short, it lacked articulated units. Articulation could only be achieved by montage, by a cutting into the undifferentiated cinema that he likened, not only to reality, but to an infinite shot sequence, a metaphor for the filmic writing of reality. This cutting on the part of the filmmaker was essentially different than the reliance upon the language system (*langue*) by the writer since natural language already possessed lexical and phonemic units as its signifiers, whereas the filmmaker only had reality and a set of historically formed stylistic conventions to work with. The filmmaker had first to create units of articulation (signifiers) from out of the indifferent mass of reality or out of cinema, the written language of reality, that was like reality though one step beyond it, or, in a slippage of likenesses, out of the infinite shot sequence, and then articulate these into concrete and significant images in a film. The cutting into reality was a cultural and thereby historical intervention, not culture naturalised but nature culturalised.

The notion and practices of the shot sequence were crucial

for Pasolini's formulations. The shot sequence, likened to the infinitude of reality needed to be ruptured in order to make reality significant, to make it conscious, to articulate it.

The shot sequence as practised in actual films, in the concrete utterances of cinema, is never infinite but part of a system of differential shots. Nevertheless, for Pasolini, the shot sequence however practised or however conceived was the reverse of the direction of his cinema semiotics and of his films, because it naturalised culture, was mere duplication even if only partially so, and thereby not articulation nor understanding, but instead a deceitful naturalism.

The problem of the shot sequence for him was that it seemed to abolish the difference between reality and the image of it and therefore made impossible any negotiation between the two, the image of reality and the reality of the image. It was the gap between these, their difference, that he stressed rather than their continuity and apparent transparency.

Language of course is based on systematic differences. Pasolini constructed a composite system of analogies whose particularities and differences were never effaced. The shot sequence for him was condemned because it abolished these differences, collapsed image and reality, and thereby eliminated the terms that enabled analogies to be formed at all whether of the kind: 'the language of reality' and its likeness, the 'written language of reality' or of the kind, in *Il Vangelo secondo Matteo*, where Calabria is made to seem like ancient Palestine and Calabrians like the people of the Bible. The particular reality of each position and their differences were made evident in the comparison. In *Mamma Roma*, Ettore is compared to Mantegna's *The Dead Christ* and the wedding banquet of whores, pimps and thieves to *The Last Supper* of Da Vinci. In *La ricotta*, Stracci on the cross is likened to Christ on the cross, specifically a Christ on the cross in the paintings of the Deposition by Rosso Fiorentino and Pontormo, the low like the high, the profane like the sacred, the real like the image as if in a maze made of reflecting distorting mirrors.

The Pasolinian analogy was seldom an isolated instance in his films or in his thought, but the very principle of their construction, a juxtaposition and confrontation of reiterated differences. The likenesses are at once like and not-like: unlike in order to construct a likeness; like in order to perceive their difference. The efficacy of the system depends on a basic difference (and accord) between language and reality, like each other and unlike each other. It is the similitude and difference between an image and the reality it represents that is the stake in Pasolini's analogical formulations.

Pasolini was particularly critical of post-war Italian films one of whose principal figurations was the shot sequence, a relatively long slice of time and space where temporal and spatial dimensions remained unified, that is, not subject to being divided up and elided. In other words, it was the real unarticulated and as such it diminished both language and reality. The double diminution was inextricably connected, and in a manner that collapsed their difference and made it imperceptible. The difference ensured that both terms would have force.

If the practice of long takes can be thought of as a characteristic of Italian neo-realism, it was not exclusive to it. It marks the films of Jean Renoir, Orson Welles, Max Ophuls and others before the war and is widespread afterwards, in Europe as well as in Hollywood, along with the use of depth of field, a mobile lens (the zoom), the moving camera (pans and tracking) and later Cinemascope. These cinematographic procedures are the hallmarks of modern cinema. Their use tended to lessen the importance of editing in a film, since a single depth of field shot or a tracking shot included what previously had been accomplished by a series of shots linked together in succession by editing, the basic pattern of which in the 1930s was a master shot and then smaller shots derived from it and dependent upon it. One of the consequences of this new development of greater mobility and temporal unity was to put into question the shot heretofore thought of as the principal unit of all films.

In the classical system, the shot was essentially a spatial unit. In the new system, the shot sequence is a temporal unit that includes a variety of points of view and perspectives as opposed to the individual shot which has a limited, unitary framed view. It was this spatial position of the shot in the classical cinema that became temporalised, causing a disintegration in the unity of the shot and its displacement by a space-time duration, not simply a new shot, but an entirely new way of constructing a film.

The shot historically makes its appearance with editing. It is not the shot that brings editing into existence, but the reverse. The unit of the shot is a consequence of editing, notably in the work of Griffith. As the need for editing changed so too did the status of the shot. A lengthy tracking shot rapidly shifts points of view. The tracking shot by its alternations in perspective, and the depth of field shot by its overlapping of spatial planes, are complex shots containing multiple and heterogeneous views.

It could be argued, and was argued, that the conventions of filmmaking in the 1930s referred to as classicism provided a false or illusory continuity. Though space and time were severely elided and sequences composed of many shots (fragments of a fictional whole edited together to appear unbroken), the joins between the shots were based on accords and a linearity that gave the impression of a unity and continuity when in fact the opposite was the case: the apparent continuities were constructed on discontinuities. In this kind of cinema, the reality of the image and the image of reality that it represented were seemingly perfectly matched. Indeed, the match cut and the symmetrical shot/ counter-shot were the main principles of classical editing. The invisibility of joins produced a false continuity as if reality and image were one, or more radically, as if the image ('writing' for Pasolini) had disappeared behind the action it represented.

One of the advantages of the new techniques that began

to be used noticeably after the war, and is coincident with Italian neo-realism, was that it produced a more fluid film, narratively, dramatically and psychologically and for some a more realistic one since what occurred before the camera could be shown not only in its durational and scenic entirety but also in its multiplicity.

The classical film is essentially based on a successive relation between shots whereas a filmmaking composed of lengthy moving shots and shot sequences concentrates less on shot relations (the shot is effectively dispersed in time) than on the relations of persons and objects in a duration within the shot. Classical editing tended to centre and create hierarchies and significances based on details, each of which was rendered in the unified shot while the editing moved from one significant dramatic element to another, the logic of action and the logic of shots in harmony. The openness of the new filming was less singular, less underlining in its effects, and less dependent on action. It was more factual than interpretative and thereby what was filmed and projected was more diversified.

What came to be important were elements associated with filming, the *mise en scène* of performance, design, improvisation, immediacy, circumstance, atmosphere rather more than elements belonging to editing, the *montage* of cutting and pasting after filming, though the distinction is not simple: all films are edited and a *mise en scène* is already a choice of relations, editing by other means. The new tendencies were promoted in the name of a new realism, though for Pasolini much of it seemed to relate to a recycled naturalism and he opposed it.

Of the various consequences of the new emphasis on filming, three might be stressed.

One, what was represented on the screen was not always clear in its relations because it was not centred and because the openness and inclusiveness of the shooting enabled multiple and differential elements to appear. It was not a realism that was most evident, but a labyrinth. The new images of the new realism were often opaque, difficult, enig matic and uninterpretable as in Roberto Rossellini's films.

Two, because the image was problematic, dramatically and narratively, the overlay between image and reality characteristic of classicism, in effect the transparency of the image, its effacement before what was represented, no longer held, and image and representation tended to separate out, exactly the disjoin that Pasolini emphasised by his contrast between cinema and film. Besides, editing never disappeared from the cinema nor could it, but now the repertory of short fragments and longer and fluid shots that were brought together made shots of all kinds more noticeable by their contrasts and differences set side by side in films; in other words, it brought the image to the fore and loosened its match with what was represented. The image gained autonomy.

The shot sequence was primarily an addition to the conventional ways of filming, and though Pasolini condemned it, it never existed alone or exclusively. It was only one type of filming in a mixed use of editing and filming procedures. Even when it did stand alone, as in some films of Andy Warhol and Michael Snow, it was as a shot not as a vehicle of representation (the disjoin between shot and representation in these cases was severe). The shot represented itself by means of the reality it filmed. It was not a shot representing a reality, but reality highlighting a shot. And, as a shot rather than a representation, it evoked shots and approaches that were the absent paradigms of it, directly raising questions of filming, time, space. The films were exercises in duration spatially measured: the infinite shot sequence, or at the very least a film composed as a shot sequence, but not leading to the naturalism associated with it by Pasolini, rather the reverse.

Three, this kind of filming was open to chance, to the accidental and improvisation, what the camera might pick up in a performance or an atmosphere or simply by inspiration, for example with the films of Jean Renoir and later of Jacques Rivette and equally what might be suggested by an image during editing as in the work of Jean-Luc Godard and Chris Marker. Films made in this manner were less fixed, preplanned, or dependent on a carefully worked out script or system of *découpage* where sequences and shots were laid out in advance as they were by Hitchcock. In short, these films were less finished than classical ones, were like sketches, imperfect and not always clearly developed. Besides, in a film composed of brief shots where space is the crucial element, there is usually only a single perspective. In the moving shot, the shot in depth and the shot that pans across a surface, by offering multiple perspectives over time also offers multiple directions, possible paths for a film to pursue, none of which are absolute and many of which are contradictory, characteristic of the films of Michelangelo Antonioni, for example, the sequence in the search for Anna on Lisca Bianca in *L'avventura* or Jeanne Moreau's walk in the periphery of Milan in *La notte* and Monica Vitti's wanderings in *Il deserto rosso* and in *L'eclisse*, instances open to atmosphere (fog, rain, changes in light, a breeze) and to the momentary (random sights, the appearance of an object). These are related to the *mise en scène*.

What Pasolini regarded as a naturalism and fetishised (for theoretical reasons) in the shot sequence is not borne out by the evidence of film practices anywhere. To the contrary. The new techniques that began to be used in the cinema after the war of which the shot sequence is emblematic marked a significant transformation of the classical cinema, not its continuation.

Where did the Italian cinema fit into this picture and in particular the works and ideas of Pasolini?

During the 1930s in Italy, that is, during fascism, the Italian cinema, with State support, rapidly developed. The direction of its development mirrored the cinema of France and most particularly the cinema of the United States, that is, it shared the same classicism and stylistic forms. It was a sign of the times. In Italy, in hindsight, and because of the experience of fascism, Italian cinema of the period has been viewed as conformist though the exceptions to such conformity and the excellence of so many films of the 1930s and early 1940s are too numerous for the description of conformity to be

credible. There were the films of Alessandro Blasetti, Mario
Camerini, Ferdinando Maria Poggioli, Goffredo Alessan-
drini, Raffaello Matarazzo and a tradition of light comedy
that was remarkable and comparable to the best of what was
being made elsewhere in Europe and in Hollywood in the
1930s. It was not a fascist cinema nor a cinema of conformity
but a classical one.

Classicism depends in part socially on an accord between
filmmaker and audience, filmmaker and society, the artist
and the world. That accord began to be less firm in Italy just
before and during the war, evident not only in the films that
were made (by Francesco De Robertis, Rossellini, Luchino
Visconti, Giuseppe De Santis) but in the criticism offered in
film journals like *Cinema* and *Bianco e nero* that called for a
new realism against a prevailing classicism that was rejected
as conventional, illusionistic and formulaic. This was not
only an Italian phenomenon nor attributable to the experience of fascism or to the anti-fascist Resistance, but evident
more generally, for example, in the writings of André Bazin
in the early 1940s in France and the example of filmmakers
like Welles in America.

Italian neo-realism in social and political terms offered a
new social contract and accord that was radical and oppo-
sitional to the one that had prevailed in the 1930s under
fascism. Neo-realism, in its emphasis on reality against
fiction and illusion, contested both a style and a form of
society that was linked to it. The social and political cement,
however, that briefly held neo-realism together just after
the war could not be sustained. Beneath the social accord
and its humanist and populist values, other and contend-
ing tendencies began to surface not only directed against
the accord and a political commitment by an accent on the
personal and the private, but against the social realism of
that commitment by a stress on the independence of forms
and the independence of the artist (no longer serving political ends). Artists and filmmakers at first alienated by the
fascist regime began to feel themselves separate from the
one that took its place, a modern predicament of alienation,

isolation and self-consciousness. The previous unities in any case were untenable.

As filmmakers like Rossellini, Federico Fellini, and Antonioni seemed to turn away from the social toward the personal, from the popular to the less popular, from the conventional to the new and experimental, a communist and socialist Left, represented by journals like *Cinema Nuovo* and critics like Guido Aristarco, denounced them as having betrayed neo-realism. What the Left condemned was a modern cinema on behalf of a social realist one still in the wrappings of classicism.

Within this situation, Pasolini made *Accattone* in 1959, the first of a number of very personal films with a personal politics. The assertion of the personal against the social, in the name of a lost unity, and the construction of the artist as a lone social prophet and critic is characteristic of modernism as is the obscurity and difficulty of the works produced. Pasolini increasingly took political positions that isolated him, and his films became increasingly opaque, embittered and inaccessible, certainly from *Teorema* onwards.

I think Pasolini's semiotics was an attempt to achieve the impossible and the contradictions within it are a sign of that impossibility as is his failure to appreciate another way of thinking of film and practising it, one in which the realism he said he loved and sought was being valued by very different means than his. Nevertheless, he condemned these tendencies either because they seemed contaminated by a naturalism or because they seemed vitiated by a devotion to style without an attendant social or political content; in either case, they were separated from reality as he understood it. He accused filmmakers like these as being bourgeois in a vulgar mockery of Marxism.

The difference he invoked between montage and the shot sequence was an attempt to reconcile his commitment to language and to reality and to their difference and mutual necessity as well as his commitment to a politics and society that might ensure that such differences would be sustained (differences in reality to guarantee differences in language). In the end, he became the main subject of his work with his genius its principal mark, a genius as if warranted by his isolation and sense of rejection that he both suffered and perhaps enjoyed. He held forth truths that few listened to, condemned lies that few cared about, turned his back on a false society that repelled him, that he railed against, and that he felt had ignored him, proposed a politics and social forms that were unacceptable and unrealistic, a voice crying in the wilderness. His films pushed relatively familiar narrative and representational forms into the service of the unreality of myth and allegory that he called reality. These were less experiments in film than ideological essays, fables for our time about lost realities, true of all his films, but especially evident in *Teorema*, *Edipo re*, *Medea*, *Porcile* and *Salò*, reality invoked by its absence, preserved in mythologising, poeticising, allegorising the real achieved by unreal means, pointed to by what it no longer was, paradoxical analogies in images of time running out.

Lev Kuleshov

The Kuleshov effect is the effect of desire. First the soup, then the hungry man. First the revolver, then the frightened man. First the baby, then the tender man. First the object of desire, then the desire. Pointedly, for Kuleshov, the effect of desire is unreal, obsessional, a hallucination of reality, the not-true for the true, the fictional for the real. Kuleshov (and Hitchcock) recognised what for them was the essence of cinema: the presence of desire and its evocation in the image.

Kuleshov's montage experiments demonstrated the fictive nature not of the image but, in any succession of them, the joins. A bowl of soup and the face of a man linked together created a scene of hunger. The same face (expressionless) and the image of a revolver became the face of fear. The fiction (the man is hungry, the man is afraid) effaced the join (the difference between the two shots). There was an internal logical connection between the shots but not an actual one: the man and the objects did not belong to the same temporal and spatial reality to be subsequently fragmented, and the fragments then joined together in film. The only reality for Kuleshov was that created by the editing (fictive, purely filmic).

The fiction was on two levels, each supporting the other. One was narrative and dramatic (fear, hunger). The other was formal: the joins between images that, though existing

in fact (in the film), were imperceptible on viewing. The link
between the images was dictated by a logic of a presumed
real action and a dramatic-psychological sense it evoked. The
action/drama effaced the visibility of the join. In doing so,
the action seemed objective, not externally determined, but
internally so, naturally, as if the bowl of soup, not Kuleshov,
and his arrangement of images determined the hunger on
the actor's face.

In American films, which inspired Kuleshov, things were
different. In these films, an actor and a bowl of soup or a
revolver were in the same real space and time as they would
be in the theatre. They were, as in the theatre, put-into-scene
(*mise en scène*) in order to be filmed. This real unity was then
fragmented and its fragments joined into a logical continuity. The real scene, to which the fragments alluded and
upon which it depended, was affirmed (adding to its realism)
while carefully balanced and centred in framing and in editing (attesting to its truth and significance). Every shot related
to a coherent time-space outside the frame which the shots
imaginatively reproduced – outside the frame was only off-
screen but always, nevertheless, present.

In Kuleshov's experiment this was not the case. Not only
were the joins and continuities revealed as fictive in fact
(Kuleshov's experiments were demonstrative), but the real
space of which the shot was only a fragment was equally
fictive (the action in each shot came from diverse spaces and
times; it was only the artifice of editing that brought soup
and actor together). There was no theatrical *mise en scène*.
The editing created the scene.

Kuleshov particularly designed film experiments that
divorced the fragment from a real continuous space beyond
it (off-screen). He insisted instead on the artifice (the fiction)
of the join between shot-fragments. The Americans used
reality to make fictions more convincing. Kuleshov, to
the contrary, insisted on the reality of the fiction, a filmic
creation that did not pertain to a pro-filmic theatrical reality.
Kuleshov's reality was hypothetical.

In American film practices, the joins between shots were
motivated by the narrative, that is, the succession of shots
was dictated by a logic of events and of character which the
film at once constructed and followed: for example, two characters speak to each other and as they do so, the image of the
one, then of the other are joined in alternation, the shot and
its counter-shot. The join is determined by a position interior to the fiction, not by an outside observer. Everything is
interiorised. There is no outside in this system, no other, no
externality, no difference posed against the interior world of
the fiction. Just as the join is made invisible by such interiority, the spectator is denied an exterior position in relation to
it. He is brought into the fiction, incorporated in its mechanisms, taken in hand from one action to the next, one shot to
the next. He is there, present in this joining, but nevertheless
invisible to himself as the join is invisible, brought into play
in the in-between of the shot and the counter-shot, the on-
screen and off-screen, the one shot and its successor. As the
objectivity of the narrative asserts itself against an awareness
of forms, and against the subjectivity of the spectator, so too
does it assert itself against the subjectivity and exteriority of
the filmmaker. The narrative dominates, not the spectator,
nor the filmmaker, nor even the film, but instead the illusion
of a reality, the fiction of an absence made present into which
the spectator fictively enters.

Sergei Eisenstein

The Battleship Potemkin begins with a small incident. The crew of the battleship are dissatisfied with the beef they are fed. It is crawling with maggots (magnified in close-up). This beginning is not unlike the small beginning of *Strike* where a worker's micrometer is stolen.

In each film the initial incident is built into larger and larger units ending in the one case with the uprising on the battleship, joined by the town of Odessa, then supported by the entire Russian Black Sea fleet, while in the other, the film ends with the revolt of the entire factory and the slaughter of the workers by the Cossack cavalry.

The dilation or enlargement works in various ways.

In *Potemkin*, especially, it is an explosive effect, not one thing leading to another, but rather the fact that interior to an event are stresses and strains that overextend it as if a detail condenses many things. Pressures cause these to collide, to heat up, expand, swell, blow, energise, then suddenly to ignite ('Suddenly' ...). Each image of the film is volatile, compressive ... and unstable.

While in the smallest detail (a maggot) resides a conflagration (a revolution), the revolution, the grand event, encompasses the most banal and infinitesimal occurrences.

There are four immediately noticeable aspects to this compacting and condensing of forces and their absorption and envelopment.

The first is a disparity: maggots and revolution.

The second is a construction. The events are not exactly consequential, a logic of before and after, of succession, but rather assembled, and the assemblage is made evident (not natural). What occurs may be necessary, but it is seldom logical.

The third is a binding. This is achieved by association. Associations can be distant in time and distant spatially. For example, Vakulinchuk, the leader of the mutiny on the Potemkin, is shot by an officer and becomes a detail that contains 'everything,' like the maggots (he is put on display on the shore). Vakulinchuk is fished out of the sea and lovingly taken up into the arms of his shipmates. This act, later echoed during the slaughter on the Odessa Steps when the mother gathers her son who has been shot by the Cossacks, resonates and creates other resonances, that of children to mothers, of children of the Revolution, of the 1905 revolt, itself the parent of a later Revolution (October 1917), of the sailors in their hammocks, like babies, like the baby in the pram on the steps, like Vakulinchuk lying in state. The townspeople on the Odessa Steps, including this mother, are running down the steps, helter skelter fleeing the ordered cadence of the Cossacks as they descend firing on them. The mother turns, finds her son, reverses direction, walks upwards against the flow of the others in flight (they halt) and against the Cossacks (who also halt) and she appeals to them in a moment of silence, of reversal, of an arrest and stoppage. This act is not alone. It too echoes and resonates most dramatically with the soldiers on board the Potemkin arrayed in a firing line like the Cossacks on the steps, their rifles poised, who halt, and this time, do not fire, and the uprising proceeds, the soldiers join the sailors the way the townspeople will join the ship.

The disparity of maggots and revolution belongs to an internal disparity, certainly a conflict, contained in every shot. From the beginning of the film, Eisenstein constructs series of shots along graphic lines and lines of movement. Ships, sailboats move horizontally left to right, right to left and sometimes are shot vertically downwards or vertically upwards. The same is true with the movement of crowds particularly in the case of the gathering of the townspeople around the bier of Vakulinchuk and then in the scene on the steps. The directions are crisscrossed (as with hammocks and hammocks like the setting of plates on suspended tables and suspended tables like the imaginary sailors that will be executed by hanging and the hanging of Vakulinchuk on the rigging after he is shot and before his fall and the hanging of the pince-nez of the officer who is thrown overboard and the spectacles of the woman who is shot in the eye and the waving of a lorgnette on the steps by a woman in a veil) so that a downward movement is met by an upward one and boats sailing in one direction in one shot are sailing in an opposite direction in the successive one (during the gathering of the townspeople with provisions for the Potemkin).

Direction, stasis, calm, quiet and expectation are the constituents of the final scene of the fleet sailing against the Potemkin then joining it, releasing it and the Revolution further gathers dimension thereby as it does in the entire film and as the entire film and all its events (including their depiction) come together and coalesce, not a natural unity but a conscious one ('One for All and All for One'). Each of the five movements of the film repeat each other and return to one another at different (higher) levels of scale, of elaboration and extended inclusiveness. Thus, the first movement (like an orchestral partition) is one of calm and violence and each successive movement expounds this one, as defeat becomes victory, mourning turns to joy, suppression to response and anguish to deliverance. The structure is symphonic, carefully clustered and composed.

The fourth is a matter of correspondences. There is an apparent development and continuity in Eisenstein's early films, but these continuities do not belong to a natural course of the action but rather to a correspondence between shots. The sequence at the Odessa Steps is one of the most dramatic and famous in *The Battleship Potemkin* and possibly over the whole of Eisenstein's work, but it is not exceptional in its structure compared to other sequences in that film and in other films.

The Odessa Steps sequence has a number of features relating to the organisation of time and of space dependent on procedures of montage and the composition of shots. Many of the shots are repeated so that at various points of what appears to be a natural progression the progression is reversed as surely as the mother who (momentarily) halts the downward movement of the Cossacks. The repetitions are interruptions (to action) but function as echoes of other actions, as amplifications and insistencies that thereby break with succession and any direct consequences of action.

Griffith's parallel alternations are always chronological and essentially linear. Eisenstein's parallelisms are seldom successive or chronological in this way and are not composed to the time of action (interior to the film) but by an abstract time of the film (exterior to it). Fragments (shots) are not joined to create a continuity nor do they refer to an interior unity of which the fragment is an essential part, but rather correspond to a need to demonstrate a relation or organise a significance.

It is interesting to speculate on the various ruptures or discontinuities engineered in Eisenstein's films. Griffith makes unities of fragments. He joins shots in a manner to mask or efface the join and emphasise instead a natural progression. Eisenstein proceeds by breaks so that a repetition dilates time and resists progression while correspondences and associations create links beyond time and beyond a line of before and after. And they create relations of tempo, rhythm and rhyming that are independent of action and often, as in the case of the Odessa Steps, are a marked distortion, an excess and overemphasis.

No shot in an Eisenstein film is ever complete because it reappears either analogically (babies in arms), or graphically (the clash of graphic lines), or in luminosity or by a contrast of beats and movements (the steps, the hammocks, descents, ascents). The incompleteness of every shot (just to be sure, the shot is often ruptured by a successive one, a close-up held too long, or a distant association suddenly evoked, or an action that has no logical precedent, or an action that is beyond the frame), its lack of finish, sustains it, like a held note or a memory that never completely fades from the film, and when it is met again in an echo, it is never quite the same. The echo does not conclude any shot, but reopens it, causes it to reverberate. It is a resurrection.

The reverberation, by the fact of it, is not only constructed and exterior to the action but exteriorises every shot as being at once within the diegetic boundaries of the film and going beyond it.

Every shot, sequence of shots, series of sequences and entire films have two directions. One is toward the reality it depicts and the other toward the composition and enunciation of that depiction. In practices of transparency (that Eisenstein loathes), enunciation is masked to the point of effacement. When Eisenstein writes of conflicts within shots and exemplifies such conflicts in his filmmaking, they refer to this double direction, of an interior natural logic of representation and an exterior construction that makes use of the realities represented, presses upon them, extending them and bringing them into a beyond of themselves addressed to us.

*

Strike, like *Potemkin*, is divided into five parts. These parts are held together by various means. There is, most evidently, the anecdote. Dissatisfied workers are stirred up to strike by the suicide of a worker in the factory. The occasion for the suicide is an engineered theft and a false accusation. The workers are spied upon then infuriated by a fire started by provocateurs. The workers are repressed by the cossacks and brutally slaughtered.

And there are themes such as spying, surveillance, provocation, false evidence that run through all the parts of the film

And within the themes there are motifs that are continuous, repeated and elaborated such as hiding (in barrels,
behind doors, around corners, in corridors, in rooms),
animals (the spies are likened to animals, the police behave
like animals, baby animals in their charm and innocence
are likened to children, the slaughter of the workers and the
slaughter of cattle are juxtaposed), water (puddles, drains,
swimming, hosing, dunking, the spilling of ink, the spilling of blood, the flow of the workers), the wheel (turning,
circularity, motion, arrest, production).

Though the anecdote is crucial to the coherence of the
film, it is also debased and mortified by the other means
of the film. These means create various ruptures of the
anecdotal.

There is the frame.

The frame is usually a cut-out, an extract, an excision from
the pro-filmic. The frame establishes a border between what
is on-screen, within the frame, and what is off-screen, beyond
it. This ensures a homogeneity. It implies a continuum
between the on-screen and off-screen. The one is simply a
fragment of the other as a part is to a whole. Every fragment
refers back to a unity.

There is a sequence in the film where the police inspector looks through a book of photographs of informers and
spies. On one page there are four photographs. The images
become animated and the figures of the informers emerge
from out of the photograph and beyond its frame. Later, they
will be likened to animals. An owl, fox, bulldog, monkey are
superimposed on them.

The expressions on the faces of the informers are deformed,
amplified, caricatured and then, in their juxtaposition with
animals, made grotesque. This framing and association is
not an excision from a continuous reality. There is no off-
screen to what is seen. Thus the continuity of the anecdote,
its presumed 'reality', is dismantled. Between one shot and
the other, no pre-existing unity has been joined nor can it
be said that what is framed is representational, because it is

an amplification, because it is a motif for association, and because it is dispersive, exceeding itself into other spheres. The images are like citations. They do not issue from a hypothetical reality but from an archive of forms (clowning, typing).

By mixing in the scene of the fire the exaggeration of the criminal dwarfs who ignite it and in the scene of the police chief attempting to recruit a worker as a spy, the grotesquerie of the dwarf couple dancing on a table, a natural, even documentary depiction (the fire, the workers in disarray, the distraught worker in the office of the police chief, the destruction of the building) is humiliated with guignol, exaggeration, and circus clowning, thus diminishing the anecdote. These scenes are exemplary. Nearly every image in *Strike*, certainly every sequence, brings together unharmonious, contradictory forms that correspond to no reality or at least to no coherent continuous one.

When the workers are hosed down, the image is at once real and an abstract play of graphic forms, particular to a scene yet part of an associative series beyond the scene towards transformations and recurrences involving water, blood and bureaucratic ink. The image juxtaposes incompatible elements joined in a montage of other incompatibilities and remote associations.

There are the associations.

The central montage strategy of Eisenstein is a montage of correspondences whereby elements distant in time and space and from different realities are brought together, for example, the hosing down of the workers paired to the rain flowing from the drainpipe as a worker is being beaten, and the meeting of the workers in the swimming pond paired to flows of emotion and the spilling of blood.

Though this knotting of motifs into clusters (there are a variety of these and they interlace, making the film dense) is a unifying principle of the film (necessary because the anecdote is diminished), it is also, contrarily, scattering and disseminative, not simply within the film, one cluster adhering to another at some other instance (the animal motif and its transferences is particularly striking: hanging cats, children tossed over the railings, a hanging worker, the slaughter of the innocents) and then itself breaking apart, but beyond the film. Because Eisenstein constructs images of contraries, because he weakens the anecdote, because every associative stream he constructs is disruptive of the integrity and stability of every image, and because he cultivates the incongruous and the discontinuous, the entire field of the film is opened up beyond itself as if there is no limit to the dispersion of elements and their reconstitution (temporary, fragile), nor can there be a here, a centre, an origin and then an elsewhere to it.

Elsewhere is ubiquitous.

The hanging cats, the playful children, the drenched workers, the slaughtered cattle, all are fragments, less of ideas than of sensations, part of an anecdote (the film, the strike), but details of infinite anecdotes because they are incomplete and because sensational, tactile, often physically shocking, not an emotion in the usual sense, but something more basic, concrete, more real even and, by that fact, open, the source of a resonance with the world and an awareness of our separation from it.

Sergei Eisenstein (2)

Of all Eisenstein's films *Strike* retains best of all the promise and mutual interests of the Russian cultural avant-garde and of the Bolshevik political revolution. *Strike* is both a great film of European modernism and a testament to the energies and hopes of the Bolshevik Revolution.

Before Eisenstein made *Strike* in 1925, he had worked for some years after the Revolution in theatre, primarily the theatre of Meyerhold associated with Proletkult. Proletkult was an avant-garde group one of whose activities, in fact its major activity, was theatre. Proletkult theatre was anti-naturalist, anti-dramatic and anti-psychological, that is, opposed, to the structures and conventions of traditional (bourgeois) theatre. It introduced into the theatre ideas and gestures derived from popular ancient traditions and their modern counterparts: clowning, the circus, acrobatics and the typed improvisation of the *commedia dell'arte*. Rather than following a dramatic-psychological line and encouraging an emotional involvement by the audience, the Proletkult theatre presented a theatre of spectacle, movement, contradiction, rhythm, colour, line, in short, theatre that displayed its forms as such rather than covering them over by dramatic interest. It was more concerned with the clash, movement and attraction of these forms and their per-form-ance than with the dramatic-psychological contrasts of the bourgeois theatre and its continuities, logic and illusions of a make-believe reality.

Strike was a Proletkult production whose actors belonged to the Proletkult collective. The film was made within its spirit.

Typage

The characters in *Strike* are not characters in the usual way. Essentially they are exaggerations, caricatures and in that sense rather than the actors seeking to realistically play a part, create a 'person', they act to distort, to make emphatic (over-acting), grotesque and comic (in the sense of clowning about). In its way it is an anti-aesthetic acting (in conventional terms). It is an acting of puns, jokes, useless (exaggerated) gestures and not easily confined within a logic or a clear meaning. Fundamentally, it is characterisation stripped of a psychological dimension and hence of dramatic functions and effects of realism (verisimilitude). It is not like reality, but a contrast to it.

Thus character is not formed from the inside, from the soul outwards to appearance resembling an internal state, but rather is purely external, a 'type', a persona, not a person. *Strike* is a film of such types and though the characters are cast in social-political roles relating to a revolutionary and socialist situation (workers go on strike and are repressed by the capitalists), the typing itself has as much if not more to do with the typing of circus clowns and medieval *commedia dell'arte* than it does with a political sense or more exactly the two are intertwined and mutually supportive.

For example, the types of *Strike* are workers, criminals, capitalists, police, army, politicians and in a more generalised way, heroes and villains. Almost none are individualised. The struggle posed in the film is between these types, that is, between abstractions, ideas and in the final analysis, between different forms.

As a result, the action that takes place, while fictional (however based on actual events) is two-sided. Because the actor 'plays' a role by exaggerating it, the performance is detached from what is performed because while the latter takes place within a fictional world, the former, the enactment, takes place external to the fiction. In the conventional theatre this line between drama and its enactment is blurred since the function of acting is to inhabit a character, to make it believable by making-believe, with the believable effacing the activity that created it. Typage works in reverse. It is not aimed to make believable, but to make apparent, a very different activity.

The non-diegetic

In *Strike* – and this is only a single instance among many – the various police spies are compared to animals: owls, bears, monkeys and so on. In fact, the spies are given the names of these animals: Owl, Bear, Monkey. These assignments and associations do not belong to the world of the fiction (diegetic) but to an intervention from outside that world which is marked as exterior to it (non-diegetic) and has been made by the film rather than issuing logically from within a naturalist drama of events. Thus the film stands not simply as the enactment of a dramatic story, but apart from it; it takes on the role of external commentary using the fictional elements as elements of a discourse only possible by abstracting them, making them unreal or challenging and contradicting them by allowing elements outside the drama to come into play.

Strike – and this is true of Eisenstein's films in general – is characterised by a discontinuity and lack of plot and story development in part furthered by the intrusion of non-diegetic elements within the fiction and that, by compromising the notion of story, plot, fiction (a continuous life-like drama) make the elements of story into abstractions.

Just as the characters are generalised types, each movement or chapter of *Strike* is equally a generality. It is not a specific strike nor are the characters individuals, but it is the generalisation of a strike, all strikes if you like, and those acting in it are enacting not a strike, not a specific event, but an idea.

Because the values of the film are essentially abstract and derealised because they are not held in or constrained by plot or the story values or a logical progression and development of events, the structure of the film can group ideas and images in ways that go beyond dramatic requirements: shock, abrupt changes, associations, an entry to and exit from what is fictional, the combination of heterogeneous and unfixed elements (photographs come alive, animals become human) as well as the freedom of transforming an event into a pattern, an abstract play of lines and light as in the hosing sequence that comes from and returns to different levels of reality rather than being made to conform to a single fictional reality.

Associative montage

In a Griffith film there is a strict relation between the shot and editing in the sense that each shot is a fragment of a fictional reality constructed and maintained by the editing. The fragments are fragments that constitute a whole. This results in a singularity for each shot, a single sense or content, since it is conceived as a fragment from which and out of which the film is literally 'built'. In the parallel editing of the chase and last-minute-rescue in a Griffith film, each shot is joined to the next in a consecutive alternating logic of pursuer/pursued, rescuer/victim which confirms the function of the shot in a developmental continuum.

Eisenstein transforms the shot (and montage) by making every shot not singular and narrowly directional, but divided and multiple. He does so in essentially two ways. The first is the one we have noticed. Typage and the recourse to non-diegetic interventions have the effect of destroying the unity of the fragment by fragmenting it into more than a single element and dividing it between the fictional and the commentative, the fictional and the outside-the-fiction, the diegetic and the non-diegetic, the character and the type.

Each shot has a foot in the fiction and a foot in abstraction.

And because there is no strict linearity or plot to *Strike*, these features are features of every shot which gives the shot an unaccustomed freedom to associate both within the motifs of the fiction and outside the fiction to ideas. Thus, the principle of unity in the film is not based on a logic of events but on a play of associations which are in principle open and infinite.

For example, one of the motifs played out in the film concerns animals; another concerns water. A series of transformations are effected between the human and the animal throughout the film which permits (without naturalising) the treatment of workers as animals and thus sanctions the comparison/commentary of the slaughter of animals with the slaughter of workers. In that slaughter, blood flows. The flowing of blood is associated earlier with the spilling of ink (administrative decrees, the anger of the capitalists), and this spilling of ink, like the spilling of blood to which it is associated and of which it is a cause, is also linked to the flow of water, the element in which the workers play, where they plan their strike, and what they use to knock down the foreman. It is also the instrument of their repression in the hosing sequence which, in turn, associates with ink and blood while equally transforming itself into the stream of workers who will, eventually, become the force and flow of the Revolution.

David Wark Griffith

I am writing to a rhythm and not to a plot. (**D.W. Griffith**)

The great achievement of D.W. Griffith was not this or that narrative technique of editing or shooting but his realisation (conscious or not) that the image had first to be detached from what it represented enabling it to attain autonomy and independence as an image. Autonomy allows images to be related one to another, to become 'writing', and thus to return to reality indirectly by images of it, the writing of a story with images of absent realities.

This realisation gives Griffith's films an uncertainty and fragility as if representation is made relative by the realities it can never fully grasp and that threaten its disappearance. His fictions had realistic aims achieved by unrealistic means.

The arts take you not to reality but to another world, parallel and distinct from the world whose signs call to figures and objects that the world can never reach while separating the arts from reality in order to see things better, that is, imaginatively, as if, in order to see things as they are, you have to see things other than they are, differently. The film image functions best when it makes strange what is familiar, makes unreal the realistic. It is the play 'between', in the interval between these positions that gives the image its power, fascination and energy, evident, for example, in the films of Bresson whose images strip reality down until what is left is the incontrovertible real, or with Rossellini, where reality is stark and cruel, a scandal even, because there is no commentary, no interpretation, no explanation, no before or after, no alibis to ease its reception.

What Griffith did, and better than anyone else to begin with (his great testament and failure, his most forceful striving is *Intolerance* composed as it is by the stressed distance between the form it takes and what it refers to), was to abstract the image from reality as words are abstracted from things and thereby not simply 'to film', in the sense of 'to record' or 'to duplicate', as the Lumières did and Méliès did, but to compose with what was filmed (editing, rhythm, tempo, suspension) and to film in order to compose (framing, point of view, scale, distance). Thus, while Griffith linked event to event (for an appearance of reality), he did so by linking image to image (the disappearance of reality).

The excitement and force of his parallel and alternating montage was not simply the product of a parallelism of events but of a play of appearance and disappearance, of a hide-and-seek between representation and what was represented, between images and the realities they brought to life and that they, necessarily and surely, left behind.

If it is possible to detect a rhythm of movement (of waves, of persons, of leaves in the wind, of gestures) in a Lumière film and in the choreographed acrobatics of much that Méliès made, rhythm and tempo in Griffith's films are not recorded but created, a function not of reproduction but of language, 'writing'.

Griffith was an inventor, creator and champion of cinematic forms, largely attentive, seldom negligent.

Alternating *montage* is ruled by temporal and causal rules, for example, in a chase scene or a shot counter-shot in a scene of dialogue. It is a movement from one to another within a coherently marked out space and time homogeneous to both parts of the alternation. Alternance is linear and successive.

Parallelism may be a parallelism which is chronological (descriptive) or a parallelism where there is no necessary or *a priori* linkage of succession, contemporaneity or causality.

The last-minute-rescue was perfected by Griffith in the use of parallel montage, for example, in *The Birth of a Nation*, with the ride of the Ku Klux Klan to the rescue of those besieged in their cabin in the middle of a field by angry, apparently bloodthirsty black soldiers. The suspense and excitement turn on the question of whether the Klan will arrive in time to free the besieged or will, instead, the soldiers be successful in breaching the cabin, entering it through its walls, doors, windows to slaughter those cringing and fearful on the inside. Always, with Griffith, the beginning of such scenes is broad and distant in space. As they proceed, space contracts, the room for movement diminishes, victims curl up, hug themselves in the confinement of closets (*Broken Blossoms*), cells (*Orphans of the Storm*), or at the gallows (*Intolerance*) or the guillotine (*Orphans of the Storm*).

The two principal spaces and times, that of the besieged and those besieging them on the one hand, and the Klan galloping on horseback on the other, are parallel and contemporaneous. As the Klan gets nearer to the cabin so too do the black soldiers. The alternation between these two discontinous spaces speeds up in tempo as if matching the hysteria of those inside the cabin and the anxiety of those who seek to relieve them, and, by processes of identification, with the anxiety of the audience. Ultimately (at the last minute), the rescue is achieved and with it the parallel times and spaces unified into a single space and time. The besieged are saved. The film's tempo of alternation and parallelism is brought to rest and completion, wound down, pacified.

Parallelism suspends the outcome of events. It seems to move in two contrary directions at once. There is the direction toward the end that the parallel montage brings to

fruition and the interruption and delay of that outcome by
the parallelism of the montage, that suspends and prolongs
the end with each shift away from where it is to another
space in a simultaneous time. The parallelism pulls (the
audience) in contrary directions, all the more so since the
uncertainty of the outcome is underlined by another parallel
sequence with a different outcome that occurred just before
in the film: the pursuit of the Sweet-Young-Thing by Gus,
the black soldier with the bulging hungry eyes played by a
white actor in black-face, and the seeking out of her by her
brother, the result of which is that cornered at the edge of
a cliff, her rescuer having not arrived, she plunges to her
death. A similar situation is presented by the threat to those
in the cabin surrounded by the black soldiers, but (as it turns
out), with a different outcome. The similarity is a parallelism of sorts since the one scene resonates with the other.
What happened to the Sweet-Young-Thing might have easily
then happened to those besieged in the cabin. Their rescuers
might not have arrived.

And this is not the end to the parallelisms struck in the
film. There is the scene of the daughter of the abolition-
ist/carpet bagger sexually under attack by the mixed race
Governor. She too is saved at the last-minute. If you go back
through the film, you can find other scenes, other moments
of salvation or death in parallel.

The three different last-minute-rescues (one failed, two
successful) composed in parallelism are different stories
of a similar situation with the same form, a duplication or
repetition based on fundamental discordances that parallelism exemplifies, exhausts and resolves, taking itself, taking
the film, taking the audience, to the brink of discontinuity,
rupture, crisis, anxiety and break.

Parallelism exacerbates alternation by threatening not
to provide the counter-shot, and making it appear that a
counter-shot will be impossible, that it will never come, that
to the cries of the Sweet-Young-Thing and the hysteria (*The*

Birth of a Nation is a film of trauma) of the besieged, there will be no answer, no merciful response, no counter, at least not in this world. To each of the potential victims there may only be, and in the case of the young girl, there certainly is, despair and death. When the counter-shot comes, when her brother arrives but too late, there is only the time for buckets of tears like the water the girl had gone to draw from the stream.

David Wark Griffith (2)

No perception is without memories ... (**Henri Bergson**)

Intolerance consists of four stories separated historically in time and space. The gaps between the stories are considerable. Each story was shot and organised differently and each refers to established and successful film genres: the Babylon story to Italian spectacle films, the Christ story to films of the Passion, the story of the seventeenth century St Bartholomew's massacre to French *Films d'Art*, the modern story to the melodramas that Griffith had perfected.

If the narrative elements of which *Intolerance* is composed were already familiar, Griffith's ordering of these was unique. Each story was a story of intolerance through the ages. Rather than telling the stories consecutively, one after the other where each would be coherently presented, Griffith intercut each story with the other such that an incident in one time and space would be related to (answered) by another incident in another time and space because there was an analogy of action and significance between them, a resonance and a memory. The stories were associated in this manner, as if each called up the other, ghostly traces from the past.

The relations between the stories and incidents were not homogeneous but to the contrary, discontinuous and varied. They are intercut with each other in parallel, and the lines never meet, unlike the parallelism of the last-minute-rescues as Griffith presented these in his short Biograph films and in his other major features where the space of a figure in danger and the space of those coming to the rescue finally become a single unified space (and time) as the parallel lines converge. In *Intolerance*, the counter-shot comes from a different universe.

As the Klan rides to rescue those besieged in the cabin in *The Birth of a Nation*, the linkage between the shots that constitute the parallel and alternating montage are linked to each other by an internal logic ultimately justified by the conclusion of these scenes when victims are snatched from destruction (or destroyed). The logic of the scenes comes from within the situation being described and the feelings that it evokes and inspires (of fear, anxiety, excitement). As the rescue nears its realisation the tempo of the intercutting in parallel is intensified. However extreme the gaps between one parallel line and the other, their differences are the stake in an eventual conclusion that is naturally motivated. Quite simply, one line pursues the other. Eventually, the two will merge and in so doing merge motive, logic, sentiment and action.

Clearly, it was Griffith's intention to employ this system of parallel montage for *Intolerance* but on a grander, more ambitious, and, as it turned out, abstract scale.

First, there is the parallelism of intolerance in all the stories, each reflecting on the other. Second, there is an organisation of parallelism within each story having to do with the threats to Babylon from the Persians, to Christ from the Pharisees, to the Huguenots from the Catholics, and to the young man from being framed for a crime he did not commit.

Third, the central story, the story that is the focus of *Intolerance*, is the modern one only, for only it has an uncertain outcome, a not-yet, a not-realised for it belongs to the present, not history. In the case of the others, the events are historical: Babylon will be sacked by the armies of the Persian King Cyrus, Christ will be crucified, and the Huguenots will be slaughtered. These outcomes are not reversible.

The difference between the present and the historical is used to create a parallelism whereby the historical stories, literally the weight of history, threaten the fate of the young man in the modern story, threaten, in fact, to repeat an historical intolerance and injustice in the present. The effect of this, ethics and ideology aside, is, on the one hand, to suspend the conclusion of the modern story (will the boy be saved from the gallows in time by those racing to the prison with his reprieve) or, on the other hand, to further endanger him by increasing the emotional pressure upon his situation through historical examples of defeat, injustice, victimisation and death as they are intercut with the modern story at an increasingly frenzied tempo until the historical stories seem literally to be superimposed on the modern one.

Griffith employs two distinct logics or organisations of montage in *Intolerance*.

The first is the most familiar, a parallelism based on an internal logic of the scene that grows naturally out of the situation presented and is essentially continuous and homogeneous since each parallel shot and sequence is based on a clear counter motive to every other. We see the victim in danger followed by the rescuers and then the victim again and so on, in parallel and in alternation, as if the one situation called to the other and as if the circumstance itself motivates what occurs, not an editing pattern imposed on events from the outside. This logic prevails within each of the stories, most especially in the modern story.

The second logic, always a potential in Griffith's films but only fully exercised in *Intolerance*, is an external logic, a comparative and analogous one based on the theme of intolerance between the historical and the actual, between past and present, the already achieved and the yet to take place, the certain and the uncertain (imaginary). These are relations with no natural connection.

These two logics propose two different cinemas. One, essentially naturalist, would contribute to the rules of the classical cinema that make a continuous flow of every discontinuous element of which it was composed. The other, where discontinuity and hence form would stand out, not against what was represented, but neither necessarily in accord with it, often referred to as the modern cinema.

If fathers are being sought, Griffith, like *Intolerance*, brought forth two different cinemas that have run in parallel lines.

David Wark Griffith (3)

> The reporter listens to the attendant with fearful bewilderment, and wonders how to handle such a man. Do you give him a ten-kopeck coin on your way out? He might be offended – he's an artist. Then again, if you don't he might also be offended – after all, he's a cloakroom attendant. (**Isaac Babel**)

The linkages between shots in Griffith's films are 'matched' in the sense that no matter how strained these matches may be to a point that they seem to 'jump' (*Intolerance*), to expose a gap, the continuity that underlies them is always reasserted. If shots distant from each other in the narrative are made to echo, resonate and rhyme with others that are not contiguous (a match is retarded, returned, repeated, an early motif is taken up later), such correspondences are narratively motivated by Griffith, sometimes accompanied by formal similarities of light, gesture, action, tone, framing or composition. Equally, and it can be a matter of puzzlement, though contiguous shots are not always immediately perceptible as successively related, it is a price worth the risk for Griffith in order to establish a parallelism where a join of action and significance, though perhaps not clear at first, can be built and dramatised to be all the stronger and clearer at last.

Fundamentally, then, neither the correspondences of the

kind I have suggested nor Griffith's parallelisms depart from an overall linear succession. Indeed, they depend upon it. His narrations never resist time and its continuities, however extreme his play with succession and sense. In fact, they surrender to continuity. Correspondences between distant shots (returns, memories, hidden truths revealed), the highlighting of instances (close-ups), breaks and ruptures in linearity (parallelism, alternation) do not exceed narrative and representational motives nor compromise the homogeneity of his fictional world. To the contrary.

Nevertheless ...

One of Griffith's most beautiful Biograph films is the 12 minute *The Unchanging Sea* made in 1910. Its story, set in a small fishing village, is as follows:

A fisherman embraces his wife in front of their cabin before he goes to sea. Together they walk to the beach. He fails to return. Time passes and his wife gives birth to their daughter who grows up and is married. The fisherman, though presumed dead, is alive. He was rescued at sea but lost his memory and therefore his past (wife, village) and thereby the future related to it. The wife's memory of him, and through her, his daughter's, are not, however, lost. By chance, the fisherman returns to his village on a fishing expedition and his memory is, as a result, restored. He is united with his wife who had never forgotten him.

Parallelism in the film is essentially between separate places in simultaneous times and between symmetrical themes of remembering and forgetting (the wife at home remembering her husband; the husband, far away, forgetting even himself). So powerful is the pull of memory that it seems as if it not only evokes the lost husband, but makes him reappear (a wish come true). The reappearance is at once fictive (imagined) and real (he is there), realised in fact but summoned by desire. Illusions are made to become true by their overwhelming and enduring force, transforming reality.

Each return to the outside of the cottage by the wife in the course of her years of waiting is textured with the memories of her love, happiness, parting, loss, marriage, the birth of her child, and these in turn call up and return to the original moment of loss creating a fabric of progressive simultaneity whereby each present moment resurrects the pasts it contains and is added to by these pasts. The narrative of loss that is being lived is shadowed by the 'other' narrative of a wished for, imagined return. Contrary to Eisenstein where juxtaposed images create a third term that resides in neither the one nor the other, Griffith works by accession, overlay. He tallies the 'sum' of parts.

Griffith's parallelism and the ruptures it entails in linearity are based on a double narrative, the one that is and the one that might be, the one that is real and present and the one that is fictive and hypothetical. When they come together, they do so strengthened. The fiction of conjunction, of dreams coming true, of realised desires, seems all the more convincing for the obstacles it has overcome and the anxieties it has had to bear. To the question, what if the likely (and dreaded) comes to pass? another is posed as its reponse, what if the unlikely (the hoped for) prevails? (the mechanism of the last-minute-rescue).

The beach scenes are composed of similar correspondences built by the frequent shots of the cabin and the incidents and instances that it echoes. The woman waved her final goodbye to her husband on the beach. Her gestures on the beach are repeated at the moments when the wife stands looking out to sea and in the split second just before the man returns to her at the very spot he had left. When the fisherman returns to familiar locations (beach, cottage, village), *his* memory returns and with it *her* reality returns from her memories.

The sense of return, of repetition, of a distance closed in memory and retained by memory, belongs to a progressive linearity that can be easily charted but it is a progression nevertheless that proceeds by turning back to what is imagined. It is this turning back, spurred by desire, that is the motor of Griffith's films and the source of his correspondences. His stories are never without a past structured into them, however small (familial) or grand (History). These correspondences give his films their verticality, one event is present within another, the past in the present, the phantasmagoric in the real. Though each shot and image follows each other in a horizontal line of consequence, they also travel vertically toward correspondences in the depths of memory and history.

The power of *The Birth of a Nation* rests not simply in its forward progression but in the density of its associations.

The New York Hat is another Griffith Biograph film from 1912, 16 minutes long. Its story is as follows:

It begins with a deathbed scene of a mother dying. At her bedside is the husband, the daughter, a priest, a doctor. The dying woman entrusts a bequest to the priest asking him to buy the daughter little feminine fineries that she might want, but to do so discreetly (secretly).

The daughter, looking in the mirror, does not like her shabby mean hat. She asks her father for a new one. Her father, miserly and miserable, ungenerous of spirit as he is of purse, meaner than the hat she wants to replace, rejects her request. The girl in turn is shunned by other women who have finer hats than her mean one. These women however desire ever more beautiful and elaborate hats than the ones they have. One in particular attracts them, a new arrival from Paris in the milliner's shop window. The priest buys the hat for the young girl, and tongues wag, especially when the girl shows up in church wearing the lovely hat.

The gossips spread the word to the respectable church committee and to the father of the girl. He returns home, seizes the hat, destroys it and berates his daughter. The girl runs off to the priest in her distress. The committee members spy on them together and imagine ... well you can imagine what they imagine. And then the father arrives filled with similar imaginings. But the letter of the mother with the trust of the bequest, words from the grave, is revealed.

Two stories have run a parallel course, the one intercut with the other: the false story thought to be true by the committee and by the father, and the true, secret story impossible for the mean-minded, jealous and miserly of the town to imagine. With the reading of the letter everyone is reconciled. Only one story survives.

Father and the mean hat are associated as are priest and the florid, alluring hat and thus the real father is displaced by an imaginary one, even though a priest. The scandal of the priest and the girl imagined by the women of the town and the father is a scandal because the priest is a priest and scandal because the priest could be a father. The survival and relief of the one story (the true story, the real story) are conditioned by dangers of these imagined stories one more terrible than the other.

The Adventures of Dollie, made in 1908, is among the earliest films Griffith made for Biograph. It tells the story of the kidnapping of the little girl Dollie and her subsequent reappearance.

The events are roughly as follows:

Dollie and her Mother are sitting by a lake. A Gypsy comes along to try to sell the Mother some baskets. She refuses. The Gypsy tries then to snatch her purse but the Mother prevents him and he attacks her. The Father arrives and beats up the Gypsy who returns to his camp. The Gypsy decides on revenge. Dollie, left alone for an instant, is kidnapped by the Gypsy. The Father and others give chase. The Gypsy takes Dollie back to his camp. He hides her in a barrel and when his pursuers arrive they cannot find her. The Gypsy and his wife place the barrel with Dollie inside it on the back of their wagon and leave camp. As they go along, the barrel falls from the wagon into the river. It plunges over rapids, finally coming to rest at the lake where the action all began. The barrel is opened by the Father and much to everyone's surprise and delight, Dollie appears.

Essentially, *The Adventures of Dollie* presents a linear series
of events. Time is successive based on logical connectives
of consequent action. There is one moment in the film,
however, when scenes of the Gypsy at home cramming Dollie
into a barrel are intercut with scenes of the Father and his
friends in pursuit. This moment aside, the film resembles
early chase films where chaser and chased are placed end to
end successively with no simultaneity posed. Time in *Dollie*
and time in the early chase films are the time of the action
within the film, not the constructed time of the film.

If, as happens in most later Griffith films, parallel alternation between simultaneous events comes to dominate,
it is always at the slight expense of linearity and a simple,
direct representation of action. Simultaneity and parallelism interrupt linear patterning, though Griffith, with the
evident exception of *Intolerance*, always restores the linearity
of time that he disrupted and the unity of space that were, as
a consequence, threatened. The reason is that these unities
and coherences are assumed from the beginning. Unities
fragmented are never lost in Griffith, but returned to and
reinstated.

The threat to these unities is twofold: that the parallel lines
will not meet or will meet too late and thus end in destruction
and also, and perhaps primarily, that the unity of the film will
be dissolved where the filmic means employed (simultaneity, parallelism, alternation by means of its montage) will not
be effaced by what they are intended to represent thus causing a sense of irresolution at the level of the form of the film
and its representational purposes. If you like, the presence
of the film might then come to dominate rather than serve
the action, intruding upon it unduly, thereby compromising
suspense, identifications, excitement and above all, clarity
of understanding (of events and their significance). This is
precisely what occurred in *Intolerance*.

Griffith's invention of new cinematic means, primarily of
montage, were stimulated by the desire to transpose the

effects of the legitimate naturalist theatre (where language was central) to the cinema (where speech was absent). Film language, as developed by Griffith, was a means to provide cinema with a voice, to enable it to speak, to comment, to render events and underline their significance, to reveal character, to evoke emotion and identification, in short, to narrate, and thereby legitimate itself as a dramatic (and novelistic) art and, equally important, as a social force.

The legitimacy of theatre to which Griffith related was a theatre of drama, psychology and character and also one of social and moral purpose. The parallelism and alternating montage he worked upon, and perfected, were means for constructing comparisons, juxtapositions and making commentary, not exclusively of events, but also of ideas and social positions that events might suggest. The excitement of his last-minute-rescues was served by an additional parallelism, namely, as moral and social commentary on action.

Embedded in the last-minute-rescues in *The Birth of a Nation*, for example, are issues of civility and barbarism, good and evil, exploited and exploiters and beyond these to a social vision and ideological import. Griffithian montage is fundamentally discursive in intent. The sentiment and emotional identifications he constructed helped to make his ideas more convincing and palatable, to make them prevail.

Griffith's discourse and the montage to realise it is not the discourse or montage of Eisenstein, but discursive nevertheless. Griffith's montage was primarily a narrative one. Each shot belonged to the unity of the narrative and the essential unity of the real that it represented, whereas in Eisenstein's discursive montage each shot is a unit in itself, assembled not in accord with an interior logic nor an internal unity, a unity already established or assumed, however fragmented, but rather by an assembly, an operation of assembling, governed by exterior reasons. Thus, for Griffith, the succession of shots (direct, parallel, alternating, reversed, interrupted) is always determined by a natural connection between them as the basis for any significance and the basis for his discourse. The procedure is essentially mimetic and representational.

For Eisenstein, on the contrary, shots and the realities they contain (and the different elements within the shot – luminosity, volume, graphic lines, directions of movement, tone) are juxtaposed without a necessary common measure between them. In fact, they may issue from separate, unrelated realities. It is in the conjunction of distant rather than directly connected realities that each takes on a new sense, is transformed, and thereby enters into new meanings and significances that separately neither possesses, for example, in *The Battleship Potemkin* in the different poses of the stone lions as if rising up (unnaturally) serving as *signs* of the hurt and revolutionary fervour of the people of Odessa as they are shelled by Czarist troops to quell their uprising, or the slowing down and repetitions of action (unnatural and imposed) on the Odessa Steps to create an emotional reaction linked to an understanding of a relation between one and all as a principle for revolution.

Eisenstein would argue that his montage demonstrated how reality worked, that is, it revealed the forms of reality, and that it was necessary to raise the image to the level of form, to understand it in its reality as form, as physical and concrete and thereby open to manipulation, rather than to consign it to a merely representational role, duplicative, mimetic and illusionary. His montage, he argued, offered the possibility of the reworking of reality in images, a possibility of transformation, of creating new realities and new thoughts, rather than accepting existing ones, as was the case, he argued, with Griffithian montage, exclusively reliant, for Eisenstein, on mimetic means for narrational purposes.

Eric Rohmer

L'image n'est pas faite pour signifier, mais pour montrer
... pour signifier, il existe un outil excellent, le langage
parlé. **(Eric Rohmer)**[4]

In a Rohmer film, characters project their desires upon what
they see. They think that what they imagine is true because
it is based on evidence. But what they see is only an image
framed (and fragmented) by desire. Reality is instead blank
and ambiguous. It is desire that gives it focus and thereby
a narrative. Rohmer edits not to interpret but to allow his
characters to do so. His shots show things but state nothing.
What is shown is the hopeless and limited attempt by the
characters to endlessly interpret in accord with their hopes.

In Rohmer's *Die Marquise von O*, the Marquise is saved from
rape by the Russian Count, her hero, the embodiment of
all virtue, before whom she swoons away. Months later she
finds herself pregnant. But by whom? Certainly not by the
noble count.

In his *Le Beau mariage*, the young woman, whose love-
making is interrupted by a phone call from her lover's
wife, rejects him in a rage and determines to marry. She
chooses, almost at random, someone to be her husband and

4 The image is not for signifying, but to show ... for signifying, there is
an excellent tool, spoken language.

convinces herself that he is terribly in love with her though he is not, gives no indication that he is, and seems hardly aware of her.

When, at last, she realises her error, the man she chose as her lover but who did not love her nor care to, falls in love with her, possibly because he is no longer loved. By then, she has lost interest.

He can't believe it.

There is always a reality in Rohmer's films other than the one that the main characters have invented for themselves and that they live. That reality, at once present yet unacknowledged (and thereby absent), though not exactly out of frame or off-screen as it is out-of-narrative and uninterpreted, appears at the close of the film to mock the story that has been lived and thereby to both diminish it because it is not true and to celebrate it because it is a good story. It mocks it by revealing that there was, after all, no story while celebrating it for its inventiveness. It is a story seemingly based on nothing but the desire for it.

Rohmer works in long takes most of which consist not of action but of dialogue. His characters speak incessantly and it is their dialogue that he films. In the fictions that they construct with their words they become their own heroes and heroines. There is no truth to their stories and without it, the characters have no roles except imaginary ones. The story they live as true is essentially nowhere, made of nothing.

There are two off-screens, one consisting of what is imagined and fictional and the other consisting of what is not understood and yet real and present (though a presence unavowed). Between the one and the other is a dialogue of invention (of a story) and denial (of what is there). Dialogue in Rohmer's films oscillate between these two positions. Each depends upon the other in a double negation, a fiction based on the denial of reality and a real based on the denial of fiction.

The mutuality of denials establishes both terms.

In Griffith, parallel lines create suspense realised by an

editing that organises and escalates the parallelism. Short shots follow each other whose contrast, rhythm and duration give his films their intensity (time is seldom real time in a Griffith film). In Rohmer, both lines of the parallel are absent, the one because it lacks reality (there is only the desire for it to be true), the other because there is no story to be told (which is the truth). In his films, the time of his sequences tends to be real and lengthy (the time of a dialogue as in Hawks). Nothing is intensified by the editing nor artificially dilated. Instead things are neutralised being no more than they are.

Since the story invented by the characters is based on nothing, nothing is the reality that they need to renounce in order to secure the story they tell themselves and that they believe to be true. Parallelism is out of the question and so too are suspense and intensity. Instead, Rohmer's characters enter a labyrinth of appearances where it is impossible for them to find their way. Where they are is always, interminably, elsewhere.

Because it also rests on a paradox, Godard's use of citations is somewhat akin to this. In *Bande à part*, for example, the entire film cites a period in France of the 1940s (Queneau, Bréton, *film noir*, the musical). The characters are not only citations from that period: Odile (a Queneau character), Arthur (Rimbaud) but they look back to it nostalgically (they are citations who cite) as if they want to be elsewhere, to live another time as the film already has them do. What is cited is exterior to the film and what the characters cite is exterior to their present, but since the texture of the film is made of this material, as are the characters, the film appears to be, and they appear to be, outside themselves so that any inside (the fiction, for example) is its own exterior, in short a citation.

Alfred Hitchcock

We travel in space in the same way we travel in time, as our thoughts and the characters' thoughts also travel. They are only probing, or more exactly, spiraling into the past. Everything forms a circle, but the loop never closes, the revolution carries us ever deeper into reminiscence. Shadows follow shadows, illusions follow illusions, not like the walls that slide away or mirrors that reflect to infinity, but by a kind of movement more worrisome still because it is without a gap or break and possesses both the softness of a circle, and the knife edge of a straight line. Ideas and forms follow the same road, and it is because the form is pure, beautiful, rigorous, astonishingly rich, and free that we can say that Hitchcock's films, with *Vertigo* at their head, are about – aside from the objects that captivate us – ideas, in the noble sense of the word. (**Eric Rohmer**)

In *Vertigo*, James Stewart's look is as important as the figure of Novak whom he regards and who he transforms by his desires: it combines the objective (the object seen) and the subjective (the manner of seeing it). The Hitchcockian system of shot (object) /counter-shot (look) needs to be considered in this context. What is seen traps the actor's look (Novak in *Vertigo* and the neighbours in *Rear Window*). It is important that the sight seen has in it something out of place, out of true and the normal, which engages the look of the character and lures him or her into an imaginary. In that sense, every Hitchcock film is a story of itself, how its fiction is engendered.

Primarily Hitchcock's films and the suspense central to them involve a perversion of the normal, a flaw in the everyday rather than what had been the classical suspense derived from Griffith, the chase and the last-minute-rescue. Griffith's suspense requires parallel times and spaces that are intercut. Hitchcock's suspense occurs in a single homogeneous space and time that, nevertheless, by the counter-shot (the symmetrical opposite to the shot), opens up a contrary, the other side to what is seen, and that Hitchcock manipulates to create a lack of balance, a derangement while remaining rigorously objective.

The performance of Hitchcock's actors is not an issue, or at least less of one than the performance of the camera and the work of editing that spies out and constructs instances of abnormality to highlight them. This is unlike the Kuleshov look that hallucinates desire in a simple countering of shots. Rather, it is a matter of rhythm and duration, in other words, of the intensity of a look (of the character and of the camera), subject and object overlapped.

Every image in a Hitchcock film has a double aspect. Seldom is an image what it appears to be, either to the principal characters or to the audience. Both are lured, fascinated by a defect in what they see at the other side of the image, no longer simply objective but overcome by emotion. Even the most documentary, plain and seemingly innocent Hitchcock image contains something disquieting and unsettling. In *Vertigo*, in Madge's studio and in Elster's office, an initial ordinary frontality and symmetrical balance in the framing and editing of shots becomes distorted, askew, unbalanced and imperceptibly so, less perceived than felt. Inside the objective image is another, a passionate one, that erodes objectivity but depends upon it.

His images have a spatial aspect that invoke an off-screen

that is threatening (the birds in *The Birds*) and a temporal one that concentrates and intensifies the image (when will the birds attack?). One takes the image beyond itself, the other condenses it, internalises it. Together time and space threaten the characters, closing in on them, no matter how, why or when they turn and twist. In *Vertigo*, the scene of Scottie waiting in the hotel room for the hoped for trans- formation of Judy into Madeleine just before she returns from the hairdresser is emblematic: the off-screen presence of her return and the waiting and expectation of it stretches time to a breaking point, making it as unreal and intense as Scottie's fantasy. Scottie is in another world whose dimen- sions are out of the ordinary.

What Scottie is waiting for is the effacement of Judy (who is herself) and the resurrection of Madeleine in her place (who is his fantasy), desire transforming reality, in this case literally. That desire (and hers to please him) seals Judy's fate (she will die, will indeed be effaced). Transformed into the false Madeleine, Judy must die (as the real Madeleine did and whose death helped to sustain Scottie's obsession) as the fantasy, crime and guilt that provoked the death of Madeleine are exposed. In the end, reason is restored, Scot- tie freed from his illusions and the world normalised.

Hitchcock's films are directly addressed to his audience. It is not only Scottie who is subject to illusions, but also the audience that is not simply watching a fiction. It, like Scot- tie, inhabits one. When audience and character are restored to reason, the film can resume being what it objectively is, a fiction, and they can resume what they objectively are, an audience and a character, no longer inside (subjective and subjected), but outside at last (watching, objectively and at peace).

The problematic, insecure, doubled, relational nature of the Hitchcock image transforms it from being the self- evident image of the classical cinema where time is linear and progressive and actions clear and transparent and above all singular into the heterogeneous image, divided and uncertain of the modern cinema, duplicitous, shifting,

lacking firm ground and questionable. The image is not
the bearer of an action (the impurity of illustration), but as
Rohmer said, the embodiment of an idea and the form of it
(the purity of cinema).

The last-minute-rescue is emblematic of the films of D.W.
Griffith. Editing in such sequences by Griffith is organised
as parallel and alternating moments between the victim and
his or her rescuer. The shot and counter-shot are images of
action. In Griffith, off-screen is incorporated directly into the
editing: a shot of the victim, then of the rescuer riding to the
rescue or a shot of the pursued then the pursuer, the counter-
shot always being an off-screen of the shot where spaces and
times are distant, but not, as in a dialogue or scene where
space is contiguous and time homogeneous, the first attack
of the birds against Melanie on her boat coming back to
Bodega Bay, a perfect example of space closing in and time
stretched in anticipation.

Suspense in Griffith is a matter of uncertainty: will the
victim be saved and the rescuers arrive in time? The excitement and expectation is intensified by an acceleration in
the editing as time is expressed in shorter and shorter shots
and rhythm reaches the equivalent of a crescendo in music.
As time is compressed, spaces are foreshortened: rescuer
and victim move closer to one another, as distant spaces are
drawn nearer by time.

In Hitchcock what comes into play between shot and
counter-shot is the look as in *Rear Window* where the fore-
shortening of space (a distortion) is a matter of a perverse,
secretive, voyeuristic look through a camera lens that brings
the distant close. The effect of the overlapping of spaces near
and far, looking and looked at, objective and subjective, shot
and counter-shot, concentration and dispersion, slows time
and distends it, breaking down natural time and space into
an imaginary, hoped-for (or feared) subjective time and
objective space of looking by the character and the audience.
In this instance none of these categories are secure and yet
all are evident.

Hitchcock has taken the central feature of Griffithian time where action is paramount and transformed it into a time where looking is paramount. For Griffith, action is speeded up in the editing; for Hitchcock, the editing is not straight-forward nor based principally on action, but instead imposes a varied emotional rhythm based on the expansion and contraction of time related to internal states made concrete in the shot of a regard rather than simply and singly an external situation. Hitchcock: 'To contract or dilate time, is this not the first task of a filmmaker? Don't you think that time in the cinema ought not to have any relation with real time?'

In *Vertigo*, Judy is the double of Madeleine Elster, while the character of Madeleine-Judy is doubled as Carlotta Valdes who the false Madeleine further falsifies by feigning that she knows nothing of Carlotta who improbably inhabits her and supposedly lures her toward suicide, but a suicide feigned, the masquerade for a murder. Carlotta's fate in fact awaits Judy once she is unmasked as not-Madeleine causing her to suffer at once the fate of Carlotta and the fate of the real Madeleine, two absences whose shadows haunt the film.

In pursuing the phantasm and labyrinth of false fictional projected identities, Scottie loses touch with himself and loses his way. His obsession divides him between a normal self and an irrational one. The entry into irrationality and vertigo is prepared by his pursuit of a criminal over the roofs of San Francisco at the opening of the film and the guilt and death associated with it when the policeman who accompanies him falls to his death trying to rescue Scottie; Scottie's pursuit of Madeleine-Judy (a criminal) is analogous to the first experience of the chase across the roofs, but the second one is more interior. Its duplication will free him from the disabling consequences of the first (his vertigo) and that made it impossible for him to save the false Madeleine. It is the awareness of falsity and obsession that liberates him. The pursuit of the first criminal and of Madeleine-Judy in her various guises opens Scottie to an adventure and the irrational where guilt and death will overshadow him and be repeated and then finally release him.

The mechanisms of doubling and redoubling take Hitchcock's characters out of themselves and their daily lives (dull, logical, passionless) into another self and a more exciting life (dangerous, irrational, fictional, imaginary, erotic, passionate), for example, in *To Catch a Thief* where Robie has to relive his past as a cat burglar in order to free himself from it; and in *Notorious* where Alicia places herself in danger by marrying a Nazi in order to spy on him for the American government and redeem her irresponsible past; and in *North by Northwest*, when Thornhill inadvertently and then purposefully becomes Kaplan.

In *Vertigo*, Scottie had lived in a normal time, carefully measured and ponderous, that he was unable to fully commit himself to, a time without intrigue or eroticism or interest. Once he enters into the irrational and imaginary, time for him and the audience becomes dense and impassioned, the world is transformed and intensified, sadistically by Hitchcock, and made exciting.

Hitchcock's journeys for audience and characters are essentially internal (structured by fear, guilt, desire). For Hawks they are external (matters of action, gesture, performance). The itinerary mapped by Hawks is determined by a logic of action and of images that impose themselves upon a disorderly world from which Hawks wrests values and sense. For Hitchcock, the itinerary of desire is mental and projected. It transforms a natural world into its opposite, the negative of it. This 'other' side to which Hitchcock leads his characters and audience is irrational, subjective and stimulating, not bound by logic but made fluid by associations.

Hitchcock's films are films of horror and humour: humorous because they are improbable; frightening and terrifying because they seem true. The audience, like the characters, is its own double, one part believing and caught and the other part laughing and observing. *North by Northwest* is a perfect example of the staging of implausible plausibilities.

The film begins with Roger Thornhill becoming other than he is, against his will, but then playfully, wondering at his own impersonation even as he suffers (and comes to enjoy and master) its consequences.

Some are born great, others have greatness thrust upon them.

Godard contends that what you remember of Hitchcock is not the stories or the succession of events or their motives (why Janet Leigh stops at the Bates motel, what Montgomery Clift stares at in silence, why Teresa Wright is still in love with Uncle Charlie, what Henry Fonda is not entirely guilty of, why the American government has hired Ingrid Bergman to work for it), but objects (a glass of milk, a handbag, the blades of a windmill, a ring, a bunch of keys, bottles of wine, a musical tune, a pair of eyeglasses, a hairbrush).

Objects have a double importance. They are the motive for scenes of suspense that they intensify. Scenes are built upon objects and the desires that centre on them – the Kuleshov effect – and all the more so because they are obdurately realistic. It is from the base of such realities that Hitchcock makes the fantasies he creates believable. The other reason is that the objects are simultaneously within and outside the narratives that contain them. On the one hand, they are a touch of realism that belongs to the narrative and objectifies it (the reality of the birds) and on the other hand, the beginning of an associative series that goes well beyond the narrative, the series, for example that touches on doubling in *Vertigo* where the narrative, rather than going forward, turns and re-turns back to itself, twisting and spiralling, as Rohmer remarks. This happens too in *The Birds* where an associative train is constructed of the birds, Melanie, the mother, spying, voyeurism, and a severe disruption of the normal which spins out of control going around and around. It happens too in *Rear Window*, a film Truffaut said was essentially about marriage: Grace Kelly flashing a wedding ring across the courtyard to James Stewart looking at her through his binoculars. Aren't all the scenes he spies on variations on a theme of marriage? It is with the object, that Hitchcock 'opens' up his films, detaches its movements from a straightforward narrative logic and action, the classicism that he belongs to and betrays.

Hitchcock's films are linear and not, transparent and not, naturally motivated and not, logical and not, centred and not, clear and not. It is the 'and', the negative conjunction that is important. By it, Hitchcock's cinema becomes a matter of questions and provocations, not answers and resolutions.

*

Hitchcock: 'In order that the spectator can fully appreciate the abnormal, the abnormal must be presented in the most realistic way. Because the spectator always knows if something is true or not true. If the spectator begins to ask himself questions concerning the implausibility of some details, that reflection will be disquieting. As for me, I will then not be able to create suspense. It is very, very important to achieve real suspense. For that, it is necessary that there be nothing at all in his mind save the suspense.'

*

Interviewer: 'In North by Northwest and Strangers on a Train, how is it possible that the hands of the heros can withstand the pressure of the feet which are crushing them?'
Hitchcock: 'I will show you. Stand there. Put your hands down. I will place my foot on them. But be careful, I weigh 220 pounds. When I have to deal with these kinds of questions, I have recourse to an old maxim of mine: nothing in the world is duller than logic. But logic is Mormon logic. Do you know anything about the Mormons? When their children ask them difficult questions, they respond: 'Buzz off.' There is something more important than logic. It is imagination. If I first think of things logically, I can't imagine anything. Often, when I am working with my script-writer, I present him with an idea. He responds:

'*Ah! It is not possible!*' But, the idea is a good one even if the
logic is not good. Logic, throw it out the window!'
Interviewer: 'What then is the fundamental logic of your films?'
Hitchcock: 'To make the spectator squirm.'

Samuel Fuller

Les jeunes cinéastes américains n'ont rien à dire, et Sam Fuller encore moins que les autres. Il a quelque chose à faire, et il le fait, naturellement, sans se forcer. Ce n'est pas un mince compliment: nous détestons les philosophes manqués qui font du cinéma malgré le cinéma et y répètent les découvertes des autres arts, ceux qui veulent exprimer un sujet digne d'intérêt par un certain style artistique. Si vous avez quelque chose à dire, dites-le, écrivez-le, prêchez si vous voulez, mais fichez-vous la paix. (**Luc Moullet, *Cahiers du cinéma*, n93 mars 1959**)[5]

Some of the leading young American filmmakers of the 1940s and 1950s, Orson Welles, Anthony Mann, Nicholas Ray, Joseph Losey and Elia Kazan, had come to the cinema from a theatre background that had been radicalised in the late 1930s where visual values and 'reality' rather than the text and the word had become most important. This theatre was 'open' to the political and social, that is, it brought into it and on-stage the immediate realities of the world off-stage,

5 The young American filmmakers have nothing to say, and Sam Fuller, has less to say than the others. He has something to do and he does it, easily, effortlessly. This is no mean compliment: we detest unsuccessful philosophers who make cinema despite the cinema and repeat the achievements of the other arts wanting to express a worthy subject in an artistic way. If you have something to say, say it, write it, preach it if you like, but leave us alone.

interrogating these elements rather than seeking to resolve them. It was as if the world had entered the theatre. If the visual and spectacular elements of this new theatre came from the popular arts, its commentative, discursive aspects came from the novel: John Dos Passos, William Faulkner, Sinclair Lewis.

The combination of a theatre of a radical, often disjunctive and excessive *mise en scène* with a political and social realism was not only disruptive of the established forms of theatre, but exposed the theatre to the unfinished, unpredictable and not easily controlled aspects of what was beyond the stage and exterior to a performance, however interiorised (real emotion), one of the rules of Lee Strasberg's 'method'. What could not be easily governed became a principle of staging and of these, two in particular need to be stressed: improvisation (an opening up to chance) and collage (different material from different sources – the real/the fictional, the felt/the false – set side by side often in relations of discord, imbalance, contradiction, inconsistency, contrast). It was not that this theatre was less formal in its concerns than the theatre it was displacing, but rather that the nature of its forms was disruptive and thus rather than simply being assumed and then exercised, it placed forms into focus and into question giving this theatre an experimental edginess characterised by roughness, lack of finish, occasional obscurity, and disjunctiveness.

It was these aspects of theatre that the young directors brought to the cinema and transformed it thereby. You have only to compare the balance, harmony and lucidity of Ford and Hawks against the explosiveness, disharmony, and lack of clarity and completeness in the films of Welles and Ray, and, also the films of Anthony Mann and certainly in the work of John Cassavetes.

Samuel Fuller came to the cinema not from theatre with its cultural and literary resonances, but from a world that was more crude, more direct and less cultivated, the world of tabloid journalism and mass media sensationalism. Fuller worked in tabloid journalism from the age of 12 years old, eventually becoming a reporter, then a crime reporter.

This kind of journalism is one of impact, emotion, explosiveness, exaggeration, lack of subtlety. It is untutored, without finesse, conservative and often reactionary. The directors, coming from the theatre, who entered the cinema came from a theatre that was left-wing, progressive, and close to the American Communist Party. Fuller's work is either militantly apolitical – 'Don't wave the flag at me' – or anti-Liberal, and extremely conservative though not in a pious homespun way which seeks to return nostalgically to a non-existent cosy past, but something more coarse, harsh, vulgar and more existential.

If a tabloid newspaper is compared it to a 'quality' one like the *New York Times* or the *Guardian* or *Independent*, the immediate visible difference is the uniformity of typeface and the balance of layout in the quality press against the lack of uniformity and imbalance in the sensational press where headlines in extreme bold scream out and where the layout is geared to impact, extremism and shock (and often extreme opinions) and where positions rather than being argued are visually asserted, provocative and didactic rather than reasoned and open. Not only are these tabloid papers arranged visually for outrage and clash and even offence (typographical shifts and variety, an apparent lack of order and harmony) but there is no categorisation of material: *faits divers*, documents, news and advertising side by side, scandal and fact together. In the quality press, content is emphasised and the style of the paper relatively unobtrusive if not invisible (like classical film editing). In the tabloid press, the style is the content as if what is important is less the news than the image of it and its amplification.

The tabloid press, in crucial, but seemingly contradictory directions, can be linked with aspects characteristic of the 'modern' arts in literature, photography and painting. What began to appear in American literature in the early part of the twentieth century in the writings of Frank Norris,

Stephen Crane, Booth Tarkington, Ernest Hemingway and especially Dos Passos was a coarse-grained realism that tended to break into the measured and enclosed fictional worlds of the nineteenth century novel (Henry James). With Norris in particular, there is a mix of styles and moods, from documentary to the grotesque while with Dos Passos, the 'real' as it enters his novels does so as part of a plurality of different discourses whose connections are obscure. This presence, often intrusive, of the document, of the real, is a new element in fiction and appears in it as if unfictionalised, 'unfitting', a jarring, discordant note and thus, to stretch a point historically, what is of the moment is less the reality than the stylistic of it which becomes evident because it is a new element and because it jars, thus opening up the novel as an exercise in style primarily as if what you are reading is more a writing than it is a content, exactly the situation with the tabloid press.

Dos Passos (and the films of Welles) present differing views of the same situation often through distorting lenses or mirrors not unlike the dual strategy of cubism that brought into its collages bits and pieces from the real world as stylistic and compositional elements, while in its paintings it super-imposed different spatial views of the same object, multiply-ing and repeating the object, disintegrating it on the one hand and reconstructing it as these disunified fragments on the other. The multiple views and perspectives that resulted were more 'true' than any singular view, while the fact of this truth was uncomfortable, obscure and distorted, more 'true' perhaps and more real as well, but less realistic. What is interesting about Welles's films from this perspective is less his use of depth-of-field and sequence shots than his editing of these in combination with other stylistic features, not this or that element, but the juxtaposition of differences.

The tabloid press presents a hyperreality as if it is not real-ity that is its reference, but rather its image, distortions and enlargements, the unnatural style of it. Fuller's films, and *Forty Guns* especially, have this quality of a reality so extreme

that, like Pop Art or a cartoon, it comes away from the screen
to appear less as reality than as an image, particularly because
Fuller in his attempt to make more real, uses techniques of
shock, distortion and disruption that call attention not to
what is represented, but to their manner of presentation.
Fuller's films are intensely realistic, but with an intensity
and amplitude that unsettles their realism.

In *Forty Guns*, Griff Bonell and his brothers Wes and Chico
are out on a road in a desolate landscape stretched across the
cinemascope surface of the screen. A dark cloud hovers over
the landscape and their buggy. Griff is coming to Tombstone
to arrest a man with Wes as his second-gun back-up. Chico
is to be put on the stage to California. Into this landscape,
literally cutting it in two and into this project, cutting it in
two, is (first heard like a thunderous rumble then seen like
a fairytale vision) Jessica Drummond on her white horse
followed by her dragoons of forty riders all at a gallop.
This explosive assault returns to calm just as suddenly as
it arrived. It is a repetitive pattern in the film of stretching
things to breaking point then ending them inconclusively to
come back to a period of unstable peace.

The three brothers then arrive in Tombstone. What follows
is a bath scene that is odd, inventive, unfamiliar and comical.
In a brief few moments later, Jessica Drummond's crazed
brother Brocke comes to town, shoots the (blind) marshal
and shoots up the town (interupting the Bonells in their
bath). The Bonells have not entered Tombstone, it seems, but
a bedlam of insanity and violence where identifications are
difficult, patterns hard to discern, where no positions hold,
where rational projects are made ambiguous and uncertain
and often dangerous (marriage, love, order, security, trust,
affection, family ties, vows).

Fuller seldom shoots a scene in medium shot that might
allow for an orderly montage of more or less similar dimensions of counter shots that classically take an audience into
a fiction and make it part of it (suturing). His scenes are

primarily shot with a moving camera, tracks, pans, zooms (like Welles and where the notion of a 'shot' becomes questionable and indefinable) in long takes varied with close-ups, sometimes extreme, especially in cinemascope reminiscent of the super westerns of Sergio Leone (unnatural, spatially disruptive close-ups of eyes, hooves, boots) and long shots from a considerable distance which function less as establishing shots than as elements in a spatial clash (long shots to close up, intense movement to calm, shots of long duration against short shots and then the reverse of these patterns).

This manner of shooting has a number of consequences. First, it helps create a permanent sensation of unease and explosiveness. Nothing you see is developed. Instead, it is disrupted and not only by acts of gratuitous and sudden violence (the shooting of the marshal, of Wes at his wedding, the hanging of the sheriff, the sweeping past of Brocke when he gets out of prison tracked with an astonishing physically breathtaking shot), but by a clash of spaces, for example, in the final stand-off between Griff and Brocke where the moving camera shifts to become at once excessively subjective and distant (the situation at the opening with the ride of the dragoons around Griff and his brothers) and the extreme close- ups of Griff's eyes, that distort space, extend time and refashion shapes. Second, it lends itself to one of Fuller's favourite figurations involving off-screen space, the sense that outside any space is another that might suddenly, and almost always does, disrupt whatever is or had been. Third, the variety and discordance between shots and scenes and the fact that they are amplified excessively results in a real so exessive that it becomes abnormal and infernal.

What was important to French *Nouvelle Vague* critics of *Cahiers du cinéma* in the late 1950s and early 1960s about Fuller's work is its stylistic extravagance combined with its obscurity, even the absence of any obvious thematic other than one related to that extravagance (disorientation, lack of identity, irrationality, insecurity, insanity) and the impossibility of imaginary, fictional identifications that made of

Fuller's films a battleground of tones, colours, movements, shocks that resonated with some of the most important artistic aspects of modern painting (the exaggerations of Pop Art, the immediacy and violence of Abstract Expressionism) and the American novel (Dos Passos, Norman Mailer).

As with Nicholas Ray, Fuller's achievements, however much one can link his work with the other arts, were specific to the means of cinema to which he brought an entirely new dimension of pure style, writing with images, in his editing and his camera (like a gun).

Bang, bang.

Dziga Vertov

In the films of Griffith, each shot belongs to the unity of the narrative and relates primarily to principles of imitation (mimetic). The succession of shots in a Griffith film is fundamentally determined by a natural connection between the shots. The determination therefore that governs the relation of shots is internal to the narrative. Each shot is of a fictive reality that has a common measure between them. Even if Griffith plays with the gaps between shots as he does in an alternating parallel montage of the two sisters separated from one another in *Orphans of the Storm* (tantalisingly close but terrifyingly far away) and in the last-minute-rescue, which is the penultimate sequence of the film, this parallelism is formed on the basis of a continuity. In a Griffith film, everything is noteworthy in the sense that everything you see relates to the narration and the world it constructs (it is economic and significant); everything is part of the same fictional and naturalised reality however distant in time or place and everything belongs to the totality of that reality.

In the discursive montage characteristic of Eisenstein's films, the linkages between shots are not primarily determined by an internal unity or an interior logic. For example, if we take the final scene of the slaughter of the workers by the cossack cavalry in *Strike* juxtaposed with the slaughter of cattle, the alternation and parallelism is of a completely different order than the last-minute-rescue in Griffith or the comparison between the two sisters at different locations because the Eisenstein logic is external and essentially intellectual. It is not an editing of likenesses (naturally generated and linked) but an assembly or construction of differential realities that have no natural similarity in time or place, instead a connection that is conceptual (unnatural). All the shots, then, are differentiated one from the other and it is in the juxtaposition of their differences that an idea is born (slaughter, men as animals, the flow of blood) in turn built up in an associative way throughout *Strike* (water, animals, flowing, streams) and beyond these to formal associations by graphic connections (the play of lines and the interweaving of rhythms as between the hosing down of the workers, for example, and their slaughter in the tenement, and prior to that, the organisation of the lines of the factory).

By juxtaposing realities that have no common measure between them, each takes on a new sense, is transformed by contact and thereby enters into new meanings and significances that neither has by itself but only attains in conjunction. You can see immediately the greater apparent openness of this constructive, assembly, mounting procedure of Eisenstein compared to the natural logic inherent in the editing characteristic of Griffith, for in Griffith's case, the narrative motivates the connections between shots whereas in Eisenstein's, the connections are outside the narrative (or can be). If, in Griffith, the differential placement of the two sisters in a context of two different worlds and two different sets of values is potentially dispersive, as if the film could fall into the gap between its differences, these differences nevertheless are made to cohere because they belong to the same level of reality.

In Eisenstein's *Strike*, the characters are types and the action that is described is also typed and generalised. Every particular instance belongs to a general and exemplary idea of it (Strike, Exploitation, Repression). Thus, each element refers to things outside the film (Workers, Revolution,

Capitalism) and because these are underpinned by units
of difference where the differences are crucial (Animals *vs*
Men, Slaughterhouse *vs* Repression), the bringing together
of these differences as comparisons (ideas) bring together
realities that are on the one hand associated in the film
(water, animals, circles) but also associated outside the film
(Revolution, Repression, Revolt). And since every element is
also an idea of it or relates to clusters of associated ideas and
themes we are no longer in a world of represented realities
but a universe of ideas about reality. Thus, the image is not
a window onto the world but a commentary upon it.

Whatever else we have said about Eisenstein that places his
films outside a conventional narrative framework because of
his discursive concerns, it is nevertheless undeniable that his
films are narrativised, tell stories, involve settings, costum-
ing, actors, performances, in short, a *mise en scène*. If in the
intercutting between workers and cattle being slaughtered,
the cattle being killed are taken from documentary footage
(found and possibly not shot by Eisenstein or if shot, shot
as it occurred, not particularly staged for Eisenstein to turn
slaughter into an image), the shots of the workers are not
found material but staged material (for the camera) as are
all the exaggerated, caricatured, 'expressive' performances
and expressive settings of the film. Before filming then (the
pro-filmic), what is to be filmed, is organised, made into a
scene (*mise en scène*) and put into play (*mise en jeu*).

The Man with the Movie Camera has a number of features that
have similarities with Eisenstein's approach but is markedly
different from it.

If montage is important and crucially so in an Eisenstein
film (as it is in Griffith), the montage (in both cases) occurs
not only 'after' the filming (true in all films) but it in part
dictates the filming (absolutely in the case of Griffith, impor-
tantly in the case of Eisenstein), that is, the organisation of
montage precedes the *mise en scène* and the shooting. What is

put in the scene and what is shot of that scene is planned to accord with an organisation of shots in the editing. The editing, thus, while subsequent to the *mise en scène* and shooting in the chronology of production is prior to both in the conceptualisation of the film.

In the case of Vertov, the opposite occurs. First, there is no *mise en scène*, no play, no scenario, no set up in the usual sense. Things are shot as 'in reality', fundamentally found material and not organised in the first instance. The shape of the film comes from the editing, but the editing does not predetermine what is shot. Instead, the editing is there to make what is shot visible, or more visible. It is a form of framing, highlighting, starring, and above all, of bringing out, of revealing the visible.

Vertov's material is more heterogeneous and more actual (more fact, document, and less narrative) than the material of an Eisenstein film (material shaped for a discourse and for a story). The 'realities' from which the images of Vertov's film come are distinct and different in time and place and in their relation (or lack of relation) to each other. It is the film that creates relations and in such a manner as to emphasise these differences (gaps, what Vertov called, using a musical analogy, 'intervals') and construct associations between them like waking, movement, silence, calm, work, leisure.

In the slaughter sequence in *Strike*, despite the differences between what is paralleled (human slaughter and animal slaughter) the narrative of the workers' strike central to the film is sustained despite ruptures to that narrative (the cut away to the cattle being slaughtered). Such linearity is relatively coherent and sensible (dramatic and expressive) in Eisenstein but is made impossible by Vertov.

No fiction or drama can be sustained against the insistence and pressure of the heterogeneity and reality of his material.

In his film, one shot does not 'answer' another (shots are not bound) but instead functions to highlight the gap and interval between them. This is made particularly acute in the 'sport' sequence and also in the sequences of leisure on the beach where every reverse shot literally reverses the direction, sense and location of the preceding shot and while we can understand the shots as 'about' leisure or movement (their commonality), they are perceived in the differences between them (their non-linearity and non-accord dramatically). Other devices of mirroring, of repetition have a similar disjunctive effect, the main result of which is to make clear the central difference of the film between what is represented and the image of its depiction, between reality and image. This gap or interval is the centre and source of the movement and interest and energy of the film.

Every shot of the Vertov film creates a doubling whereby you see an action in the image simultaneously with seeing the action of the image and this goes so far in the film as to present you with the projection of a film whose subject is the construction and viewing of it: reality and image as both different and comparable, whereby the image, the shooting, the montage are placed in a relation to what is shot (the real) as not only different from it but capable of seeing beyond it to something that for Vertov was more real and true than any conventional (natural) view.

His construction (montage) is an organisation of the visible. This organisation of the visible (constructed, exterior) is what makes the visible visible and not a *mise en scène* or *mise en jeu* which artificialises and fictionalises it.

By creating an assembly (not a unity) of entities Vertov creates an open rather than a closed construction. The construction is based on the discontinous and the different and opens these to a continual flux and possibility of association, repetitions and variations of the same and their differences by different juxtapositions. Eisenstein, though working in similar ways, has a stronger narrative line and fictional setting. Certainly, his images are less free and less mobile.

Every movement in a Vertov film makes clear a double determination, as an effect of action (a horse gallops, a cart goes by, a train passes, an athlete leaps a hurdle) and an effect of film (action can be stopped, movement reversed, the train is being captured on film, actions are repeated, mirrored, doubled etc). With Vertov, it is a film that is passing by, not simply a buggy.

Howard Hawks

All films, perhaps, and the best ones especially, are a response to the questions: what is the cinema? what is its essence? what can it do best? The films of Howard Hawks do two things best. One, they can capture moments and instances that no other means but the cinema can do as well, and in the cinema, few can do that as well as Hawks: a movement, a glance, an action, the immediacy of a gesture and their direct honesty. For example, John Ireland's readiness to spring in *Red River*; the tension in Montgomery Clift in the same film when he draws on Wayne and opposes him for the second time (the first when he was a boy); and also in *Red River*, the look of surprise on Wayne's face when Joanne Dru addresses him by name at the encampment. And other examples would include Bacall's sinuous joyful walk of freedom through the hotel, counterpointing the music and flowing with it at the close of *To Have and To Have Not*; the softness and challenge in Angie's Dickinson body when she dares Wayne to search her in *Rio Bravo*; the shimmering of the light on the water as the cattle cross the river in *Red River*; the dingy feel of the streets, offices and roads in *The Big Sleep*.

Two, is to tell a story well: directly, simply, coherently, legibly, to take an audience with you, making perceptions and understandings clear and secure. Hawks tells his stories in such a way that the development of events seem natural and organic without anything to disturb their continuity or unity (nothing fancy, abrupt, inexplicable), allowing for the special moments of intensity and graceful beauty that the camera can catch and the editing underline and then retire. It is a matter of *mise en scène* and of editing with only a hair's breadth between them, each serving the other and hardly distinguishable.

'I dread editing' (*'J'ai horreur du montage'*), said Hawks. If a film is shot badly, if the *mise en scène* is poor, it would be evident at the stage of editing and no editing could then save a sequence. Hawks dreaded editing, not as an activity, but because it would reveal to him what had gone wrong in shooting. The *mise en scène* was an opportunity for montage and montage the realisation of the *mise en scène*, bringing it out. For Hawks, montage was not a time for improvisation, play, unlike shooting or working with actors and preparing the script. The best moments of the film had to be found in these pursuits before montage. Besides, *mise en scène*, for Hawks was already an understanding of ordering of shots. 'But don't you edit your films?' 'I edit as I shoot, if possible, but editing as such is a drag.' (*'Mais vous faites le montage de vos films?' 'Oh oui! en même temps que je tourne, si possible ... monter est un pensum ... '*).[6]

When one part of the Hawks film asserts itself as style, punctuation, forms, it is only to herald the entry of the other: the story, intrigue, characters. Neither the film nor its style is so insisted upon as to disturb the story but its preeminence is a matter of style. Hawks's style is modest, self-effacing, efficient, and though acting effectively on behalf of the story, is not simply its illustration. What an image shows (the action it describes) and to which its composition and sequencing and the entire architecture of the film contribute are so complementary that any difference between them is almost imperceptible. The content of the image includes the way things are presented and how they work.

6 Jacques Becker, Jacques Rivette et François Truffaut 'Entretien avec Howard Hawks', *Cahiers du cinéma*, n56 février 1956.

Montage for Hawks has two distinct but not contradictory functions. The first is to highlight (dramatise) and the second is to move forward (a logic of consequence).

In the sequence in *To Have and To Have Not* of Bacall and Bogart skirting around each other, going in and out of their rooms, a sequence that mirrors a similar and earlier one between Cary Grant and Jean Arthur in *Only Angels Have Wings* in his room and in the hotel bar and also similar and later scenes between Bogart and Bacall in the Greenwood house and then in Bogart's shabby office in *The Big Sleep* and between Angie Dickinson and Wayne in *Rio Bravo* in his room and her room in the hotel and at the bar, create a balance and harmony in the exchanges between the characters and between the shots (length, point of view, framing, centring, lines of force) such that a move or stress in one direction is answered by a contrary move or direction in another, and so tightly-knit as almost to overlap. Nothing is without its counterpart that binds (as consequence) and stresses (as emphasis) at the same time.

The sequences are fragmented, moving from one detail to another, one figure to the other, one glance to another. Words cover the movements and punctuate them, not the source of what is going on, but belonging to it, part of its unity. The fragments, characters, looks, movements, expressions, voices, actions, all belong to different registers, but all so perfectly linked and harmonised, so naturally motivated, that the fragments are effaced for the unity that they constitute and to which they belong and to which they return.

Just as every encounter, violent and not, by words or deeds, by dialogue or bodies is choreographed by Hawks, so too are his images precisely orchestrated, at once for dramatic effect (where time is intensified and its progress resisted) and for continuity and flow (where time and action move forward). The moments of intensification occur when everything seems to stop and continuity is halted, particularly true of the action sequences that simultaneously bring the film along and stay the film in that place, like the murders

of Canino and of Eddie Mars in *The Big Sleep*. Every moment
is part of a continuity and springs beyond it.

In *To Have and To Have Not*, the relation between Bacall and
Bogart and their individual characters is played out around
cigarettes, on lighting them, smoking them, exchanging
them, searching for a match. When Bacall and Bogart are
cornered in his room by the Sûreté Nationale and Bogart
plays a game of cigarettes with Bacall in order, unobtrusively,
to reach his revolver in the desk drawer enabling him to
shoot one of the police and regain control of the situation,
the previous plays with cigarettes give his movements their
purpose, naturalness, effectiveness and deadliness. They
prepare Bogart, prepare the audience and prepare the film,
and they do so in unison.

Bogart's movements are improvised and deliberate, immediate and controlled, exactly like Wayne's movements in
the shoot out with the three deserting cowboys in *Red River*
when Brennan throws Wayne a rifle as he had thrown him
a knife in an early encounter with an Indian. The care and
inventiveness with which characters act, as if every moment
is a danger and every danger an opportunity (your life is at
risk but so too is its value – are you good enough?; when
Dean Martin in *Rio Bravo* wheels around and shoots the
killer hiding on the landing), are qualities not only of the
characters but of the films.

    What Hawks values and respects in his characters informs
the way he shapes his films: with attention, concern, cour-
age, professionalism, skill, a sense of ends to be achieved,
and the wit, grace, honesty and invention to achieve them.

If his heroes acted differently, they would be defeated or die,
and if the films were made differently, they too might die. In
a Hawks film, the value of life is affirmed in its fragility and
by its strength, and by a sense of peril to overcome and then
the joy and satisfaction in having succeeded (Barthelmess
landing the damaged plane and redeeming himself in an

action, wordlessly in *Only Angels Have Wings*). For his characters, risk is always present, and everywhere, and in the smallest details. Hence, the need to attend to these details.

So too with his films.

Howard Hawks (2)

Between 1926 and 1970, Hawks made 22 films, one of which was in Cinemascope: *The Land of the Pharaohs* (1955).

Cinemascope, like depth of field, sequence shots, lengthy tracks, pans and the use of the zoom reduces the need for editing. Rather than fragmenting space, space can be left relatively whole and time can be given its due, the time of an event being simply the time of the shot, hence the length of takes with these new techniques (the opening of Welles's *Touch of Evil*, for example, and the scene in the hotel lounge near the beginning of Visconti's *La Morte in Venezia*). André Bazin would argue (rather too sweepingly) that such techniques rendered the real more fully than did montage and that rather than breaking the real up for analytic and dramatic purposes as he claimed montage did, the real was left in its integrity.

What Bazin had done was to notice a shift in the technical means of the cinema and to register its aesthetic consequences that seemed to him (correctly this time) to redefine the cinema, though Bazin, wrongly and misleadlingly, gave this redefinition a metaphysical sense. For him, it was a restoration of the real in all its fullness (untampered with, unmanipulated), its mystery (sacred) and its ambiguity (nothing pointed to, selected, interpreted).

However wrong Bazin was in his metaphysical conclusions, he had recognised an important historical change and one that divided the cinema between a 'classical' one and a 'modern' one, not, as he would have it, a cinema that put its faith in the image (montage) and a cinema that put its faith in reality. What the new techniques resulted in was a relative lack of centring in the shot and the dissolution of the wholeness of the shot as it was understood and used. The shot began to be reconceived and realised in a variety of new ways and with it so was montage. Ambiguity was an aspect of these new techniques not because the real was ambiguous, but because the changed manner of shooting created a multiplicity of perspectives, framings, distances, points of interest whereas previously the shot, so crucial to the editing patterns of the 'classical' cinema concentrated interest, centred upon details and by forcing the spectator into a position thereby secured his understanding. This is quite different from the effect of long takes and a moving camera in the films of Welles, for example, the Venetian fortress in Cyprus in *Othello*, becomes a labyrinth of corridors, walls, depths, rooms, as does Xanadu in *Citizen Kane* and the Luna Park in *Lady from Shanghai*. It is very difficult to argue that the effect is one of greater reality; on the contrary, these views are perverse and opaque.

Essentially, the montage techniques of the Hollywood cinema that Bazin objected to for its intrusiveness and undue shaping of reality, its violation of the real, and, in effect, its falsifications and illusionism, was concerned with making clear, with providing perspective, with unifying, and thus enabling an audience to follow events without undue difficulty. This cinema was concerned with legibility and comprehension and what went along with them, excitement and drama, for which a coherence of action, of detail, of space and of time were essential elements, all the better achieved by the control and accords made possible by carefully linked continuity editing, so an audience would always know where it was and things were. Quite simply, you could link essential details in a logical continuum. This cinema was not principally a visual one (the visual is often ambiguous, puzzling and even opaque) but a cinema of readability (whose virtue was clarity).

Curiously, the shot, in the classical cinema, no more than a fragment of a whole, the master-shot with which scenes and sequences usually began and just as frequently ended, was not eliminated by these new techniques any more than was montage. Instead, the shot was called into question and its functions changed. For example, in a lengthy track or a depth of field, how could you define the outlines of a shot that constantly redefined itself in space and in time? Indeed, it could be argued, and the films of Godard perfectly confirm it, that in the new cinema that developed from the early 1940s, the shot becomes more important, however differently conceived, than it had been in the classical cinema, the cinema that Hawks perfectly exemplifies.

In the classical cinema, all the elements with which the shot was composed – planes, spaces, depths, sound, dialogue, movement, perspective – were joined narratively and dramatically. But as these objects and purposes became less important, their constituents in the shot became more independent of each other, as in the films of Bresson, relatively indifferent to narrative purposes, and as in the films of Cassavetes in such a way that the shot begins to dissolve, divide, disperse, bifurcate, as in the films of Godard, Marker and Resnais.

The shot sequence, so dear to Bazin, because of its wholeness and the unity of the real within it, has a complexity that the smaller, fragmented shots of the 'classical' cinema lacked. The purpose and practice of that cinema was to link certainties and to make certain. Though the sequence shot does not fragment the consistency of the real, the ambiguity of it and the uncertainty of what it is that is significant, and the twistings, turnings and meanderings of the camera, as in the lengthy tracks through empty corridors in *L'Année dernière à Marienbad*, or in the streets of Hiroshima in *Hiroshima mon amour*, or the wasteland of the concentration camps in *Nuit et brouillard*, are not only unclear, even opaque and whose sense is difficult to find (the shots are decentred and narratively unfocussed), but in part, and because of that lack of focus and centre, they give the impression of unreality as in a dream with odd connections and odd shapes and perspectives. That is, the more techniques employed that seem to ensure the integrity of reality, the less real do things seem to be, for example, the chateau in Marienbad, the death camps, the city of Hiroshima. This loss of clarity and readability, however, has resulted in a gain in visual qualities. But this must not be confused with reality any more than should the depictions of the classical cinema.

In Hawks's 1956 interview in *Cahiers du cinéma*, just after the appearance of his *Land of the Pharaohs*, Hawks had this to say about Cinemascope:

> *Nous avons passé tout notre vie à apprendre comment obliger le public à concentrer son attention sur une seule chose. Maintenant, nous avons quelque chose qui fait exactement le contraire [Cinemascope], et cela ne me plaît plus beaucoup. J'aime ce procédé pour un film comme La Terre des Pharaons, où l'on peut profiter pour montrer beaucoup de choses, mais je ne l'aime guère pour les histoires habituelles. Ce n'est d'ailleurs pas difficile, c'est même plus facile: vous n'avez plus à vous inquiéter de quoi que ce soit, vous avez tout dans le champ. Je trouve que c'est un peu grossier. A partir du moment où vous utilisez le Cinémascope, vous ne pouvez plus monter rapidement, vous perdez donc un moyen d'excitation, un moyen d'augmenter la tension dramatique d'une scène. Vous ne pouvez plus conserver le même tempo: c'est une erreur de monter vite en Cinémascope parce que le personnage saute sans cesse d'ici à la; c'est invisible. Il faut donc procéder très différemment. Ce que vous perdez sur le plan dramatique, vous le gagnez sur le plan visuel: le résultat est plaisant à l'oeil.*

[We have spent our entire lives learning how to induce the public to concentrate its attention on a single detail. Now, we have something which does exactly the opposite [Cinemascope], and that does not please me very much at all. I like this process for a film such as *Land of the Pharaohs*, where one can take advantage of it to show many things, but I don't care for it for the usual stories. It is not that it is difficult, in fact, it is easier: you don't have to worry about what is necessary, you have an entire field at your disposal. I find that a bit crude. From the moment you begin to use Cinemascope, you cannot edit quickly and thereby you lose a means of stimulation, a means of increasing the dramatic tension of a scene. You can no longer maintain the same tempo: it is a mistake to edit quickly in Cinemascope because the characters jump unceasingly from here to there; it is invisible. You have to proceed very differently. What you lose on the dramatic plane, you gain on the visual one: the result is very pleasant to the eye.]

Jean Renoir

Je crois que ce n'est pas la seule méthode pour faire
les films qui partent au début et terminent à la fin, et
qui sert en somme comme une énorme scène. Mais
personnellement, j'aime mieux la méthode qui consiste
à concevoir chaque scène comme un petit film à part.
(Jean Renoir)[7]

As Schumacher pursues Marceau in *La Règle du jeu* during
the *fête* at La Colinière aiming at him with his revolver and
firing, Marceau hides behind various guests and servants
and 'props' in the château (pillars, corridors, doors). The
scene resembles scenes from the films of Chaplin and has
similar qualities of absurdity, play-acting, performance and
comedy. It is a precise choreographed madness in the midst
of a setting that is real and involves a drama that could be
real and in the end, turns out to be deadly. The scene is at
once farce and serious drama. The guests are uncertain how
to take the 'performance'. Does it belong to the gaiety and
play of the *fête* or is it real?

The world of the servants and of the guests, of lower
class and upper class is ruled by conventions and appearances. It is artifice that holds it together. Social reality is that

---

7 I do not think that the only way to make films is to begin at the beginning and end at the end as if it is one huge scene. Personally, I prefer a
method that conceives each scene as a small film in itself.

artifice. Nothing is as it appears to be and thus behind the
'scene', there is always something else (a repressed sincerity,
hidden jealousies, disavowed passions), that is, all that does
not conform to appearances, to the rules of the social game.
Everyone at La Colinière is in masquerade with the exception
of Jurieu, Schumacher, Marceau and Christine, all, in their
different ways outsiders to the world of the château whether
above or below stairs. The eruption of the passions of these
characters into the social masquerade of society reveals the
masquerade underlining the rules of the game in playing
against them and by their actions forcing the other players
to unmask if only momentarily and reluctantly (the Marquis,
Octave). The primary rule is not to admit that there are rules
at all but rather to make believe that the rules are reality, that
masquerade is sincerity, that artifice reality.

Jurieu lands at Le Bourget, an aviation hero. He has crossed
the Atlantic in record time in a solo flight. The crowd is at
the airport to cheer his accomplishment and heroism and
the nation is listening to the report on the radio. But instead
of acting as the social rules would have him act, he plays the
jilted lover and does so publicly on the air waves and it reaches
the home of the Marquis and Marquise de la Chesnaye. It is
for love of Christine, the Marquise, that Jurieu attempted the
flight. What Jurieu does and says (his sincerity, his passion,
his disappointment) is against the rules. He is a hero behaving
unheroically like a spoilt, frustrated child.

The film holds up a series of mirrors: sincerity to artifice,
desire to convention, the personal to the social. These not
only reflect each other, but interpenetrate until their differences are put into play, simultaneously revealed, obscured,
reversed as if each is within the other.

Most often films are thought of as representing something (a
reality or the reality of the imaginary, an idea, a significance).
In Renoir's films this is neither issue nor intention. What
artifice and masquerade display is the reality they deny and
what the reality of the film reveals is the theatre and artifice
of the rules. The one becomes the other inevitably, and the

other, the one, of necessity. Insidiously, they penetrate each other. Nothing therefore is firm and nothing can be said to be what the film represents. Instead, the film reveals, and simultaneously, a representation but as constructed and a reality that is theatricalised, at once a play and an inquest into itself, reflection and self-reflection.

In this manner, gentle, tender, affectionate, Renoir, less as an intellectual commitment and more as instinct and warmth, the lack of boundaries as a human quality, makes his film into an object, inevitably in order to reveal a certain humanity, self-reflectiveness not as an aim but as a natural consequence.

Renoir approaches reality through the openness of his theatricality (*its* reality). It is by asserting its artifice that he is able to provoke the reality that causes it to exist in the first place. This is a matter not of thematics but of method. He places his characters in a dramatic or comic situation and then follows and observes them (with his camera) rather than constructing them (with his editing). Much of what is said and what occurs is improvised at the moment. The film is the performance of the actors in a situation in which they find themselves, performance at once play and revelation, make-believe but in the quest of truth. The most wonderful scene and moment in a film of wonderful scenes and moments in *La Règle du jeu* is when the Marquis presents his splendid, magnificent mechanical toy to his guests at the *fête*, in an expression that combines pride and shyness, a tentativeness and delight. At once, and magically, the Marquis finds his true self on stage and with the help of a toy.

The rabbit shoot with its realistic detail is invaded by a drama which is a drama of appearances. Christine 'spies' the Marquis saying a final goodbye to his lover that reveals to her the game of love and the loyalties and infidelities in which she had been implicated and had believed in or was unaware of and which she now undertakes to expose. That mistake (taking appearances for reality) is a mistake that Jurieu had made (mistaking social friendship for love) and would cost

him his life (Schumacher, like Christine, mistakes a costume
for a reality and by that mistake exposes a reality hidden by
the rules of social masquerade). The instant Jurieu lands at
Le Bourget and breaks the rules, his fate is inevitable.

The penultimate scene of the film (the shooting of Jurieu,
like a rabbit) that is caused by Schumacher's error of perception, taking a costume for a reality, an error caused by jealousy and passion (mistaking Christine for Lisette and Jurieu
for Octave) resonates back to the *fête* where everyone is in
costume and no one who they pretend to be or more exactly,
are who they are despite being in costume in which they
appear not to be who they are. This too is a mirror since it is
only in costume that they become themselves whereas before
they were play-acting in the costumes of social decorum. The
final scene that converts the château into a theatre (that it has
always been but only in that last moment tragically revealed
to be) and the characters become simultaneously spectators
and characters (watching a drama interior to the drama they
have played), in masquerade and not, concludes with a social
lie to ensure a social truth: the rules of the game that Jurieu
tragically disrupted and that the Marquis restores.

*

The fluidity of Renoir's camera (the lengthy tracking shot
in *Le Crime de Monsieur Lange*) following Lange through the
offices and corridors of the Cooperative and into the courtyard that ends with his shooting of Batala, the conclusion of
a shot and of a scene in perfect harmony, the length of his
sequences (the party in *La Règle du jeu*) and the use of depth
of field photography (the rabbit shoot in *La Règle du jeu*) that
allows him to follow, observe, accompany his characters and
their actions, in contrast to the continuities established by
editing in the 1930s, particularly in American films, may in
fact belong to one another, especially since these Renoirian
attributes become more generalised in the 1940s. Certainly,
the relation between the one approach and the other should
not be thought of as in opposition or as exclusive.

Films of the silent period, with few exceptions, in part

because characters do not speak, give the impression of narratives not unfolding but of predetermination hence their dreamlike quality, the shadowiness of being since characters have no words and words thereby no determining power, no initiative in an 'unfolding'. The talkies diminish the tragic theatrical quality inherent in the silent period (the talkies are essentially novelistic). Narratives after sound begin to unfold, to develop as if escaping their former confines, while their characters have more of a role, more individuality, in short, more substance. Thus filming and editing become less a matter of shaping than of revealing, less about construction than about accompaniment, less about predeterminations than about the adventures of facing life and improvising it.

The fictionality and theatricality in Renoir's films belong to these changes initiated by the coming of sound. What concerns him is play and performance as a consequence of the freeing up of film from the tragic and the determined and it is here that reality enters not simply because of the thin line between play and reality, fiction and the real, that so concerns Renoir and that he plays with so wonderfully, but because of a new interest in watching, recording, revealing rather than stating.

It is not that the world becomes film, more real than reality, but that film loses a centre of determinations, a core around which things had revolved, and thus it becomes more mixed, more heterogeneous, more opaque, more ambiguous, more uncertain, more delightful, and, well, more open to 'reality'.

All of Renoir's films concern escape, fleeing, not exactly from society, though that typifies them often (*Boudu sauvé de l'eau*, *La Carosse d'or*), but from unnatural constraints (*La Grande illusion*, *French Cancan*). It is the spontaneity of the one and the rigidity of the other that keeps things going in his films. In the end, inevitably, the place of freedom, the place to escape to, the place of possibility and decency (not moralism) is not in fantasy, but in creation, in film, theatre, play and the delicacies of desire (*Élena et les hommes*).

Renoir is interested in how we are or might be or could be, never about what we ought to be, still less, what we are doomed to be (Eisenstein, Griffith too, Lang perhaps). The new cinema that he heralds perfectly accorded with these sensibilities.

Jean Renoir (2)

Une oeuvre d'art ce n'est pas un sujet, mais un style.
(Youssef Ishaghpour)[8]

The scene of the *fête* in *La Règle du jeu* has two principal elements. The first is the multiplicity of characters and of actions and the second, their interconnection, not simply dramatically but visually. You see simultaneous actions and diverse centres and you see them all at once either because the camera records actions in depth or because the camera constantly is in movement and though travelling in time registers simultaneities. These actions and the spaces in which they occur overlap, each embedded in the other and inextricably. The behaviour of the servants mirrors the situation of the guests and the 'play' of the *fête* is difficult to distinguish from the (deadly) reality of the intrigues of jealousy and love. Everything can be named but nothing demarcated.

In *French Cancan*, for example, the distinction on-stage/off-stage is blurred from the beginning. La Belle Abbesse/Lola is acting not only for the audience in the theatre (La Belle Abbesse), but for Danglard in the wings (Lola). It is a double performance, one regarding her 'life' or reality and the other her 'role' or masquerade. They are embedded positions shown by the shot in depth that brings together stage, audience and the wings of the theatre. The audience

8 A work of art is not a subject, but a style.

is part of the performance and everyone at once actor and audience. There is never exactly an off-stage in Renoir's films, only different levels, intensities and tones of being on stage.

The end of *French Cancan*, the performance of the cancan, the explosion of colour, movement, sensation, energy takes place not on stage but within the space of the audience (the space is cleared for the dance and for that purpose some of the audience is placed on stage). That scene is preceded by the performance of Esther Georges who sings her number within the physical space of the audience and also to different audiences. Danglard and Nini are during her performance behind the stage, divided by a curtain and by jealousy and contradictory intentions. The discovery of Esther Georges by Danglard first occurs in the dance studio where, quite casually, he hears her voice through a window overlooking the street across from the studio. It turns her singing at home into a performance, her flat into a stage and Danglard seated in the studio is as if in a seat in the orchestra without anything in fact being changed. The studio is still the studio, the flat still the flat. Danglard's discovery of the warmth of depth in Esther George's voice and in her body and person and the transformation of one space into another has a tonal resonance. It is a shift in colour between two spaces and two moods and yet it imbricates each with the other. It occurs at the moment of Danglard's most complete defeat. The loss of Le Moulin Rouge and therefore of the possibility of staging the cancan caused by the jealousies of Lola and of Walter. But the discovery of Esther Georges is a triumph in hope and a moment of joy that displaces the defeat, eradicates it in a feeling even before it is eradicated in fact.

It is the lack of demarcation, or more precisely, a refusal of it, that characterises Renoir's method: the masks that every character wears and the artificiality of their situation and performances, their 'play', that blurs the line between the theatrical and the real. Masquerade and role-playing are never made separate from sentiment and desire and yet their difference is clear.

Renoir rejects what is traditionally central to the cinema: the frame and the shot and the borders that mark their boundaries and the borders within shots between details and objects that set these off and give them a definite focus, centring and intent. Renoir tends to show things in their continuity, hence the embedding, the instability of frames and positions. He films in scenes, not shots, placing the scenes end to end not as continuities and consequences for dramatic ends so much as tonal alternations, modifiers, as in *La Carosse d'or*, where the film shifts between the space of performance on stage (ordered, formalised, brightly coloured, artificial) and the performance behind the set and off-stage (chaotic, out of control, dark, potentially deadly, 'real') or where the real is formalised in the manners and artifice of the court and equally theatricalised when jealousy and desire become elements of farce, part of the play. These tonal changes mirror one another: the commedia troupe, the world of Camilla and of the theatre on the one hand and the world of the court, the Viceroy, power and politics on the other. Sometimes the differences come together (on one or another stage) with the golden coach serving as both object and cause of these interactions, intertwinings and multiple reflections, of a hide and seek between off-stage and on, life and theatre. It is also, during the voyage to Peru, where Camilla and her soldier-lover slept.

A perfect example of this interconnectedness takes place during the council meeting deliberating on the Viceroy's request for funds from the nobility. In one room, off the main meeting room as if off-stage in the wings, the Viceroy's mistress is making a scene (a performance of jealousy) and in another room, opposite, equally off the main room, Camilla is performing her act of jealousy. The Viceroy rushes between rooms from one performance to another in order to pacify the crossed lovers and maintain the decorum of the meeting whose reason to be centres on the golden coach, an object that concentrates show and power, artifice and economy, and that sets off a train of crisscrossed, farcical jealousies and rivalries.

In *French Cancan* as in *La Carosse d'or*, the tonal shifts
between scenes are not only of mood but of colour and movement: the yellows and heavy greens of the street against
the brightness of blues and reds in full light in the theatre
scenes.

When Camilla in *La Carosse d'or* rejects Fame (the bull-
fighter), Security (the soldier), and Wealth (the Viceroy) to re-
enter the world of the theatre, and when Nini in *French Cancan*
joins the performance of the cancan having renounced Security (the baker), Wealth (the Prince) and becomes reconciled
to a rejection in Love (Danglard), it is not in terms of an
equation, art versus life, theatre versus reality, but the discovery of reality in theatre (passion, joy, acceptance, liberation,
energy) and an awareness of the theatricality of life that only
the artifice of theatre can show and put into play. Camilla
crosses the line and joins the troupe. Nini becomes aware
of the line and becomes a trouper. The awareness makes
choice possible and leads to it being made. To choose theatre (art), as Camilla and Nini do, and as Renoir does is not
a rejection of reality. On the contrary, without the one the
other is nothing.

Jacques Rivette

... je suis de plus en plus persuadé qu'il faut faire les choses faciles, et laisser les chose difficiles aux pédants.
(**Jacques Rivette**)[9]

Rivette's films are composed of scenes or sequences made up of one shot or only a few. The sequences are relatively lengthy. If Rivette wants to change an angle, perspective, distance or focus, he tends to move the camera or the lens rather than to rely on cutting. Ellipses are between sequences, very seldom within one.

After a film has been shot, Rivette views the rushes all together and all at once. He does not view them in daily bits as the film progresses. Because his scenes tend to be shot sequences, rather than being cut up into brief shots and recomposed, the work of montage for him is essentially a choice of sequences not of shots. During editing Rivette is interested to discover what a film is saying by itself (*par soi-même*) rather than what he might have wanted it to say. Montage, for him, is a seeking out of affinities between different moments of a film that exist in themselves (*en eux-mêmes*) and are there to be found and are the spirit and life

9 ' ... Increasingly I am persuaded that it is the simple things one must do, and the difficult things left to pedants.'

of a film. It is more a matter of permitting a film to take its shape rather than to impose one upon it.

Shooting and composing in sequences allows Rivette to follow the action as it takes place and develops. Because little is prearranged or foreseen, this method of filming (and editing) is designed to keep the film open, giving it air. Much of what is filmed is decided upon at the moment of filming, not *before*. There is no script that pre-exists the film and that it illustrates or represents, the film being the *after* effect of the script, but rather a script written alongside the filming and that keeps it company. The script is written on the set as things happen, each stimulating and encouraging the other.

A sequence shot is a shot of things developing in real time. Not only does Rivette employ sequence shots but he shoots his sequences sequentially in the order of the film, not for the sake of the continuity of the narrative but for the sake of the fluidity of the film. Working this way makes his films fresh, immediate, elegant and full of surprises. His method extends to the actors and acting. Actors are encouraged by Rivette to find their own direction and in relation to each other on set. The result is what engages Rivette, a result at once and free (anything is possible) and terrifying (anything can go wrong).

Nothing pre-exists the film: no script, no narrative, no plot, no *découpage*, nor do the actors mimic a preconceived character (also true of Rossellini's films and Renoir's). The film is made at the moment of its making as are the performances and the characters. The films have no strict outside (the filming) nor inside (the representation). The film is itself, not a representation of something else that precedes it. In any case, the boundary between outside and inside, real and illusory, play and seriousness, freedom and constraint are vague and fluid. It is their going back and forth and what lies between them that is the magic and fascination of Rivette's films.

Cutting in most films is essentially a cutting out of what is not interesting (weak moments) or not pertinent (irrelevant moments). Rivette does not cut in this manner ('*c'est une violence ...* '). To do so, for him, would be a diminution. Instead, Rivette adds and enlarges and by so doing, lightens the film, as if by lengthening it, it becomes more brief and tremulous. His films are very long (3–4 hours) and seem to happen in an an instant.

The strict ordering implied in cutting (certainly classical cutting) is for the most part an act of underlining (this) and thereby an act of exclusion (not that). It forces things; thus, for Rivette, it prevents them from arriving by themselves ('*venir d'elles-mêmes*'), arriving as if by accident or by chance.

In the opening of *La Bande des quatres*, Anna is found by the camera walking along a street. She enters a building, walks up the stairs, goes along a corridor into another room, takes off her coat and stands upright, immobile, her arms folded. A minute after, and through the door that Anna had entered, another girl comes in, takes off her coat in the corner and they begin to argue about lovers and constancy. Once inside the room, the sequence is substantially in one shot. It gradually becomes clear as the shot opens outwards that they are speaking lines in a play (by Marivaux: *La Double inconstance*) at a rehearsal (they are not alone) and these lines will resonate in their lives as if there is no transition between outside the theatre and within it, or, by extension within the film or beyond it as happened in Anna's entrance. These characters and their words will be played during the film by other characters as if they are interchangeable and yet on the other hand, are not, since each is trying to find her rightness for a part. The overlap and shift between roles in life and roles in theatre will move back and forth. Characters will not say or not do in life what they say or do on stage and the opposite will occur. The characters, who are doubly characters, in more than one role and between positions (free, constrained) seek out their roles sometimes in one place, sometimes in another.

Montage is a linkage or juxtaposition of differential elements and, as Rivette's films bear witness, should not be limited to the joining of shots.

Michelangelo Antonioni

In the early 1980s, Michelangelo Antonioni had three major exhibitions of a series of photographs entitled *Le montagne incantate* (The Enchanted Mountains) in Venice, in Rome and in Paris at the Louvre.

The photographs are of images of imaginary, fairy-tale mountains painted in watercolours or constructed of collages of strips of watercoloured paper glued onto a page. Antonioni enlarged the photographs and at a certain point arrested the enlargement process, printing the resulting images. These images are *le montagne incantate*.

Watercolours tend to bleed, disperse, seep and fade off as if going away from the figure they are meant to define, a transparent shadow of what they represent, without body, clear outline or substance.

The original images drawn and constructed by Antonioni are, like all images, unstable, the more so for the sketchy, fleeting, ghostly quality of watercolour. Every image of *le montagne incantate*, it seems, contains an infinity of other images as if these were, virtually, always present from the beginning with the originals and their enlargements Enlargements, by definition, contain other images of the same, smaller or larger, as if each image belonged to a series of itself.

In Antonioni's film, *Blow-up*, a photographer, by chance,

takes some photographs of a woman and her lover in a park. The woman notices the photographer and tries to retrieve the photograph from him, demanding it, anxious for it, worried about his spying and catching her and her lover unawares. Intrigued, the photographer develops the photographs he had taken, studies them and then, caught by a detail in one, enlarges it. Enlargements can go too far, expanding an image until it fragments into its constituents, like an explosion. The enlargement reveals traces of a crime, a possible murder. It 'brings out' what the original image hinted at but obscured. Before the photograph is enlarged, the evidence of the murder is imperceptible. After it is enlarged and becomes evident (or at least possible to imagine), the photographer begins to wonder what might lie behind that image (as he wondered with the original), and, as if to confirm it and nourish his curiousity and imagination, he enlarges the image further. The result is unsettling. As the first enlargement displaced the original image and revealed a murder where there had not been one, so the second enlargement displaces the first. The new second image loses the figure that had been revealed in the first enlargement (the murder disappears), dissolving it into abstract shapes and lines as if what was seen had never been (only an image after all, and thereby unreal), precisely the relation between the original image and the first enlargement, each image as if uncovering a hidden truth of a previous one. The uncovering of image after image is not a revelation of a truth or reality that the images contain but only the reality of images.

Antonioni's enlargements infinitise his images by exposing their virtualities. It is not simply a matter of scale, but of time and of definition. In the enlargements in *Blow-up* and in *Le montagne incantate*, the choice of stopping an enlargement is a choice within a series that can be made at any moment and at any point, any one of which will result in a different image, endlessly.

In *Le montagne incantate* exhibition, each image that is

shown is a moment along a path of images not shown, a pause in infinitude, rescued as an instant from the oblivion and void of virtuality. The point of hesitation of the exhibited image is crucial, it is a *between*, between the legibility of the subject and its dissolution into abstraction and informality. It recalls the wondrousness and beauty of Étienne-Jules Marey's chronophotographs, their dance of movement and light and Marcel Duchamp's time-motion painting (itself a series), *Nu descendant un escalier*, inspired by Marey, that, like Marey's experiments, contained all the phases and lines of a movement, not consecutively and separately as with Muybridge, but simultaneously, every line, all the pasts, presents and futures of a gait, gesture, flight, descent. What is noticeable in Marey and Duchamp, the transformation of figures into the abstractions of images, where truth and reality are seemingly at odds, is also noticeable in Antonioni. What Antonioni holds onto is neither the figuration nor the abstraction, but both, figuration alone being banal and the loss of it dispiriting.

At any point of these still moving images, there is everything and nothing.

In Antonioni's *L'avventura*, the disappearance of Anna on the island of Lisca Bianca to the indistinctness of the sea, or to the blankness of the horizon, or to the formlessness of weather, or to the variability and unreliability of sentiments, or to all of these, is a *between* in the film, an irresolute, vacillating border compounded of the virtuality of other images, stories, possibilities that are present without being represented (Anna has drowned, Anna has escaped, Anna will return, Sandro and Claudia will become lovers, their relation will die, disappear like Anna, drift away) and that include all the images that have gone before and those that will follow, not in a continuity, but as a virtual range, vertical like a paradigm not horizontal like a sentence or a narrative.

The final image in the film of Claudia's hand hesitating to touch Sandro after discovering his infidelity (it comes just at the moment when she believes herself most happy, always a

moment of risk), is the same kind of wavering and inconclu-
siveness that occurs in the sequence on Lisca Bianca. It also
belongs to the enigma of the photographs in *Blow-up* and
the in-between of the images of the enchanted mountains,
enchanted because they are never still, never settle, never
solidify, whose abstraction comes from figure, bringing it
out and losing it like the series of paintings *La Montagne
Sainte Victoire* of Paul Cézanne.

Because Antonioni's images are unstable, the realities they
depict become so as well (love affairs, landscapes, sentiments)
while the relations between the image and what it depicts are
exposed and made questionable. On the one hand, these are
only images (an objective enlargement but not realities); on
the other hand, they are a contemplation and investigation of
images (critical, interrogatory), and they are as well subjective and sensual (Antonioni is inside the series).

In the classical film, image and reality are fused – no
questions to be asked. This fusion gives the images of classical
films and the impression of reality they create their solidity,
hence the exemplary importance in that system of the shot-
reverse shot (the very expression of it) where every image has
its symmetrical reverse and in a horizontal line, actualised
or not. The counter is always off-screen somewhere and
that needs to be insisted upon as a real place and naturally
consequent, not an off-frame which is a constructed place
whose determinants are external to the fictional world of
the film not internal to it and necessary for its stability and
sense. The reverse shot is the counterbalanced opposite of
the original shot and functions to hold it in place making
it impossible for the shot to go anywhere but toward this
cohesive interiorised inversion. All the shots are secured and
the audience bound into their course and logic: complete,
self-sufficient, perfectly legible.

The trajectory of an image becoming other images that
displace and unsettle them by processes of enlargement
or diminution as with a zoom lens or a tracking in or out,
provides a perfect and smooth continuity uninterrupted

unlike the shot reverse-shot, but seldom results in its clarity.

The careful editing of the exchanges between Bogart and Bacall in Hawks's *To Have and To Have Not*, particularly in the hotel, between their rooms, where each image is a direct response to every other that together in the sequence of the events and the shots depicts the progress of a relation between the two central characters in a manner that is transparent, efficacious, crystalline and replete. To the contrary, the wandering of the characters on Lisca Bianca and the uncertainty posed by the images of that wandering, images that could always be other than they seem to be (and that become so) and to which there is no response (Anna has disappeared leaving a void), no accord, are on the contrary, empty, obscure, blank and labyrinthine.

Michelangelo Antonioni (2)

None of the images that are effaced by Antonioni's enlargements ever truly disappear. They make their presence felt as
phantom shadows. The same is true with other disappear-
ances, returns, repetitions and meanderings characteristic of
Antonioni's films. Anna is never more present in *L'avventura*
than when she vanishes. She haunts every subsequent scene
especially the final one where her presence is an echo or a
chord held for too long or the whoosh and whistle of a passing train like the one that interrupts Sandro and Claudia
making love in a field or the reverberating bells rung in the
towers at Noto when Sandro, unable to rid himself of the
ghost of Anna, proposes marriage to Claudia, equally unable
to free herself from the ubiquitous images of Anna. The
presence of ghosts that stalk Antonioni's films give power
to other scenes of effacement and erasure in *L'avventura*
as when Sandro overturns (as if by accident, certainly by
compulsion) the bottle of ink on the drawing done by the
young man full of hope and inventiveness as Sandro once
was in another life. And then the children parade past.

There is the same echo of a disappearance when Sandro
and Claudia come upon the newly built but abandoned town
on the road to Noto, like the metaphysical landscapes of De
Chirico.

What haunts a scene, a relation or an entire film even
in Antonioni is the trace of other paths, other possibilities,

other films, not taken but not thereby renounced. The shadows that forever return like phantasms and cannot ever be silenced deflect the path of every assertion and definition, causing these to fade, dissolve, unsettle into ghostliness.

In the classical cinema, the fragmentation of unities into morsels that then replenish the wholeness that they have broken away from is an operation of reconstitution, realignment and continuity. A shot will be responded to by another such that if a figure in a dialogue momentarily disappears as a consequence of a reverse shot, that shot in turn will be countered, and that one countered again and the figures, their presences and accords with each other re-established as a progression and without a tear.

In Antonioni's work, returns are absences.

Jacques Rivette (2)

Pour lui [Rivette], chaque plan est comme un film, avec
un début, un milieu et une fin, un déroulement, une
tension. (**Nicole Lubtchansky**)[10]

La Belle noiseuse is four hours long. Most of the action
takes place in the studio of the painter Frenhofer (Michel
Piccoli) painting his model Marianne (Emmanuelle Béart).
Frenhofer is a master painter. He has not exhibited for years.
His last work, for which his wife Liz (Jane Birkin) posed,
was left unfinished. It was *La Belle noiseuse*. Marianne and
her lover, a promising young painter, Nicholas (David Bursz-
tein), come to Provence to visit Frenhofer in his studio to
see his work. A gallery owner tries to provoke Frenhofer to
finish *La Belle noiseuse* with Marianne as his model, in the
nude, a suggestion unknown to her. Nicholas concludes the
arrangement and then tells Marianne, who is furious that he
has decided on her behalf without her consent, but resolves
nevertheless to go through with it and to model for *La Belle
noiseuse*, not to please Nicholas, but, on the contrary to annoy
and vex him (sexual jealousy, professional jealousy).

La Belle noiseuse can be translated as *The Beautiful Nuisance*.
It is what Frenhofer cannot complete and what Marianne

10 'For him, every shot is like a film, with a beginning, a middle, an end,
an unfolding, a tension.'

becomes to Nicholas and to Frenhofer. A number of deci-
sions have been freely made by the characters to see what
the consequences might be for each of them. Every character
(Frenhofer, Liz, Marianne, Nicholas) becomes a spectator of
the others and of themselves: how will Nicholas react? how
will Marianne react? what will Liz do? what will Frenhofer
do? what will 'I' do?

It is typical of Rivette's films that his characters choose to
place themselves in situations whose outcome is unknown
and for motives that are mixed and confused. Such choices
initiate and are the foundation of the fictions of his films:
the choice to pose, to paint in *La Belle noiseuse*, the choice to
save France in *Jeanne la pucelle*, the choice to return to Paris
in *Va savoir*, the choice to set up a household in *La bande
des quatres*, the choice to marry in *Hurlevant*. The action
of the films is what happens as a result of these choices.
Since Rivette's films are literally composed as they are being
filmed, the situation of the actors mirrors the situation of
the characters while the situation of the film mirrors the
situation of the action that takes place within it. The actors
are complicit in composing the roles that they play as are
the characters in the fiction. Similarly, the film seems to be
seeking itself as it is being made and goes along.

Once Marianne becomes Frenhofer's model (on a whim)
and he begins to sketch and then paint *La Belle noiseuse* (on
a whim), both are set on a course to discover things about
themselves and about each other by means of their situation (to pose, to paint), similar to the situation of the film
(to set in scene and to film). It is not clear how things will
work out or how to arrive at any ends, in any case constantly
being revised, deflected, questioned. The only way is to try
things out, day by day, sketching, rethinking, attempting one
pose, then another, one approach, then another, in the studio
and in the relations beyond them with wives, lovers, friends.
Each has to feel his or her way. The actions of discovery and
observation are the fascination of the film. Since it is shot
in lengthy sequences, often of a single or a few shots, to

enhance and make possible in real time within the confines
of a set and narrow space (principally the studio) the regarding that is central to the film, the film on the whole is thereby
relatively lengthy. Little seems to be cut out as if the film
is an accumulation of regards. The film, like the fiction it
frames, works itself out as it goes on, observing the result of
one move and then, most often, pushing it further by invent-
ing complications (obstacles, doubts, questions). This is the
other aspect of the film when a regard raises a question and
the questions (to be answered) result in intrigue, plotting,
machinations, not only for the characters, but for the actors
and the scriptwriters and for Rivette.

To choose is to choose constraints. To observe the consequences of choices is to act and it is the action that the film
follows and in following, foments. No matter how innocent
the impulse to only observe may appear, it is false, and
inevitably, a strategy of provocation and not to be trusted.
Innocence is a form of artifice and deceit, especially for a
filmmaker. The fictions that result from the play of false and
true, machination and observation (in all of Rivette's films)
are also the stories of their own inventions and the film the
narrative of its own creation.

Freedom to move becomes more and more limited in a
Rivette film, for the characters and for the film, until it seems
that there is no way out except by some act of violence, of
destruction, of deceit (lies are common and more common
is the denial of lying; this is a film after all and everything is
feigned and all truths false), up to the point when the film
has to take account of itself and the consequences of the play
of relations it has initiated and the characters have to take
similar account of the effect of the artifice of performance,
acting, plotting as a result of their apparently innocent deci-
sions to choose and their denials of deceit. It is in that play of
artifice that truths may surface, hiding something to reveal
something like Frenhofer's false *La Belle noiseuse* to cover
up the true *La Belle noiseuse* that he conceals and to cover
up the concealment. Play, deceit, the artifical are means to a
truth and to what is real. All the manipulations, scheming,

intrigue, twists and turns, the made up, the invented, the false come to be surprised, almost by accident, with the real, its object all along, but which, if artifice is taken seriously, cannot be forced or known in advance.

The cinema of the French *Nouvelle Vague* in the late 1950s and early 1960s and the critical writings of this group in *Cahiers du cinéma* had two contrary positions.

One was a position in favour of realism. The other was a position in favour of artistry (the *auteur*). It is not difficult perhaps to see why the films of Renoir, Rossellini and Rouch were so important for the *Nouvelle Vague*. All of them play with falsity and artifice as powers to arrive at (reveal) reality and all of them were aware of the shifting, uncertain border between artistry and truth in the paradox *une vérité cinématographique*, an oxymoron of an entire generation.

Une vérité cinématographique was best expressed by *mise en scène*, a compound of oppositions and vague margins.

Mise en scène was the artifice of setting something up to be filmed, and in such a way, that the filming of it would catch realities of gesture, movement, colour, sound of the scene, at once a formality and a concreteness, the cinematic and the real. *Mise en scène* was also about presentness, not exactly improvisation so much as attentiveness to the moment, film not as an illustration of something preconceived but as a seizing upon the moment that the film in its setting provoked so that the act of filming was like a writing rather than merely a reproduction. The idea was troublesome for traditional views of representation.

Hence the hostility to montage either as a pre-existing *découpage* where everything was known in advance (Hitchcock) or montage as the subsequent fragmentation of the integrity of scene, thus in either case the loss of the reality of the scene itself, of the inherent power of its momentariness, whether smooth or (more usually) awkward – *la vérité cinématographique*, often rough, of the films of Nicholas Ray, for example, or those perfect moments in Renoir where play discovers a purpose and thereby a sigh (Octave gives his overcoat to Jurieu).

The films of Rivette are magical not for truths or realities they express but for this difficult to recognise *vérité cinématographique* that they are, a path that begins simply as play (innocently) to become rich and complex, because so much is being risked by impersonation, by fiction, by not being who you are to discover who indeed you are, so much left to the accidents, chance, delight, dangers and surprises of reality that needs the help of being put into scene.

It is a matter of faith.

Alain Resnais

... nous avons l'air de supposer que la réalité existe en dehors de l'oeuvre et cela même n'est pas tout à fait sûr. Une oeuvre, c'est une sorte de conscience. Comme dans la vie courante, le monde n'existe pas tout à fait sans la conscience qui le perçoit, pour l'oeuvre d'art il en va un peu de même. Les choses racontées n'existent pas vraiment en dehors du récit que l'oeuvre en donne. **(Alain Robbe-Grillet)**[11]

The opening sequence of *La Guerre est finie* takes place at a border crossing from Spain to France, in the morning, just after dawn, on Easter Sunday. The border is marked by a river. A car is halted in a queue of cars on the bridge across the river as it makes its way forward to the French customs and immigration post. In the car is the driver, a French bookseller from Hendaye, the first French town after the crossing, and Carlos, a Spanish refugee living in Paris.

The car has come from Madrid, some hundreds of miles south of France. Carlos is a refugee from Franco's Spain and a professional revolutionary seeking to overthrow the Spanish dictatorship. He has been in Madrid for six months

---

11 ... we imagine that reality exists outside of the work, but that is not an absolute certainty. A work is a kind of consciousness. As in life, the world does not completely exist outside of the mind that perceives it and for the work of art it is a bit like that. Things narrated do not truly exist outside of the narrative that the work gives to them.

planning, with others, a general strike to take place at the end
of April. Carlos is 'Carlos' within the movement, 'Diego' to
one lover and 'Domingo' to another. He has had other names
over the years. He is carrying on this trip across the border
a false passport under the name of a French engineer, René
Sallanches. Carlos speaks perfect French and can easily be
taken to be French, or Diego, or Domingo or Carlos depend-
ing on the situation. He has different identities and different
lives, that cross, but are distinct, moving, if not in parallel,
with each other at dissimilar levels. Carlos is hoping to take
the train in the morning to Paris from Hendaye. He had
left Madrid suddenly because of a wave of arrests by the
Spanish authorities of members of his cell. In Paris, he is to
meet with the Central Committee to advise it of these recent
events in Spain.

Over the image of the car (but not of Carlos), there is a
narrative voice-over, spoken by a narrator describing Carlos's
thoughts as he waits on the bridge. The voice is that of Jorges
Semprun, the scriptwriter of the film and the author of the
words.

Just as the exterior narrator describes Carlos's thoughts
(the familiarity of the journey, the crossing, making it safely
into France), as if the narrator is taking Carlos's place, indirectly
speaking for him, another voice describes the fears during
the journey that the car might break down and not arrive in
time. That voice is, like that of the narrator, exterior to the car
(it has no face), but unlike the narrator, it turns out to be interior to the fiction, being the voice of the driver describing his
thoughts earlier in the journey. It only becomes evident that
it is the driver who is speaking and that the voice is within
the fiction when there is a shot change back to the interior
of the car and his voice is integrated with his image.

The disjunctions of the joins are disquieting as if they have
a river to cross between the breaks that separate them. The
joins, though met, however discontinuous, are also barriers,
like Carlos's different identities and different names. The
barriers (multiple identities, voices from elsewhere, voices

without faces, false voices) are marks of differences that encounter each other and seem to condense or fuse (interior with exterior, past with present, narrating and narrated) not as if there is no difference between them, but that the differences are unstable and difficult to specify or to 'hold' onto. As a consequence, these encounters suggest that within their folds or between them something has been caught and remains hidden.

What is presented by the film are fragments, not of a whole or of continuities later to be reconstituted, but kernels, nuclei of disparate, shifting, inconsistent elements that can generate others, or atomise and proliferate. Each term is like an exile, like Carlos, a refugee in a foreign land where nothing is clear and nothing what it appears to be. The lack of settlement and certainty of direction, time, place makes every shot a living thing, not tied and shackled by needs of succession, drama, sense or definiteness, 'held' in place. Instead, the shots are open to association, allusion, interlacing and the imaginary.

Wherever Carlos is, he is simultaneously elsewhere. It is the same for shots, objects, phrases, sequences. Every detail resonates with others or receives echoes from afar that transform it.

In any film, a shot change in a succession of images is a rupture even if it is used to constitute a continuity as is mostly the case. In Resnais's films continuity is almost never the object of shot changes. On the contrary, the shot change for him is an edge between differences that are marked, then used to create groupings of likenesses. No shot in his films is singular. It contains all manner of similitudes and paths and into which it can enter and depart, like Carlos, like exterior voices, like an image that then multiplies into images like it, of women, of desire, of losses.

In the classical system, the shot is effaced on behalf of the

whole into which it is integrated. The shot only has an existence in the classical system as part of a structure of accords,
but it has no independence, no presence, no power, for it
is always constrained, locked into place by the continuities
that govern it and that it serves to create. With Resnais, the
shot is affirmed in its discontinuity, thereby liberated to
join other shots without losing itself, as in a collage. The
classical film, in erasing the join between its fragments, for
the sake of succession and action gains a fiction (the fiction
of continuity), but loses the reality of itself (the reality of
discontinuity).

There are borders in Paris as there is a border between Spain
and France ... and a river as well.

For Carlos, the borders in Paris are between Nadine whose
existence he hides from Marianne and Marianne whom he
deceives; between a revolutionary life that is secret and an
ordinary one made false in order to preserve the secret, revolutionary loyalty that he betrays in his heart but honours by
his actions; and between revolutionary adventure that he
denies by his words and is frightened of and his sympathies
for it within his heart (himself as a young man); between a
revolutionary past (that is unreal) and a revolutionary present
(that is overstated). Carlos lives these states and times, each
masking the other, each simultaneously affirming the other
and denying it. His life depends on these contraries.

Nadine Sollanches (the daughter of René Sollanches (whom
Carlos has impersonated crossing into France), thus becoming fictively her father and really her lover (the fiction excites
both of them) has entrusted Carlos (her Domingo) with a
suitcase of plastic explosives from her revolutionary group
now under surveillance by the police. It is not clear whether
the police have been led to the young militants (placing them
in danger) in the course of trailing Carlos or the police have
been led to Carlos (placing him in danger) in the course
of trailing the young militants. Each group of new and old
revolutionaries, present and past, is a mirror and inversion

of the other, what Carlos once was and no longer is, a repetition that has run its course.

Marianne is the woman Carlos lives with in Paris when he is in Paris (he has been in Madrid for six months). To her, he is Diego.

Marianne and Diego leave her flat in the evening in her car to go to a film. He drives. Their car is stopped by the police for failure to turn on the headlamps. Diego presents his papers: driving licence, passport to the policeman. They are allowed to proceed with a warning. They head toward the Gare du Lyon where Diego intends to deposit the suitcase full of explosives in a left luggage compartment at the station given to him by Nadine (Marianne thinks they are documents).

In the flat, before they left, Diego asked Marianne to stop by the Gare du Lyon to drop off the suitcase. In that scene, there are three projections by Diego: one of Agnès, an inquisitive friend of Marianne, opening the suitcase, another of Lola, Marianne's Spanish maid, taking the suitcase down from a shelf, another of Diego depositing the suitcase at the Gare du Lyon. Such images interrupt sequences throughout the film as they do here, for example, during the opening border crossing sequence (imagined scenes by Carlos of his arriving at the Gare du Lyon from Hendaye, of him on the train, of him taking a lift to a comrade's flat, of him rushing to catch the train from Hendaye, of him meeting Juan ... all of these are imaginary projections).

The projections concentrate and condense distant times, spaces and images of future meetings, future revelations, fears and hopes commingled, parallel images, often unrelated, brought together. Just as Juan and Agnès can be made to meet over divides and times in an imaginary, so too can Marianne and Nadine, Diego and Domingo, or a coffin, a letter in a tube of toothpaste and a suitcase of explosives in a locker.

When Marianne and Diego reach the Gare du Lyon, she takes the suitcase from him, against his wishes, to deposit it in the left luggage compartment, pointing out to him his absent-mindedness mentioned by the policeman in his forgetting to light the headlamps. Earlier, when retrieving the suitcase with Nadine, Domingo reminds her of her absent-mindedness in failing to light her headlamps and she questions him about his documents just as the policeman questions him when he is with Marianne and earlier still at the border crossing (where Nadine, on the telephone confirms to the police inspector, Carlos's false identity as her father, René Sallanches).

Diego follows Marianne at a distance into the station and watches her deposit the suitcase. He is in the same position as the policeman who had followed Nadine and Miguel from the cafe 'La Chope' and whom Carlos follows in turn as wary revolutionary and perhaps too, jealous lover. As Marianne approaches Diego, they walk together side by side and she seeks his hand. They hold hands as Miguel and Nadine did walking side by side with the policeman and Carlos behind them.

It is not only imaginary images that meet in the film but images of action and gestures that associate as likenesses and returns as if time were circular.

La Guerre est finie has a number of themes and conglomerations: exile, deceit, hiding, meandering, falsifying, meeting, appointments, telephoning. Appointments are kept (the time of trains, of border crossings, of Central Committee reunions, of seeing Roberto), not kept (Andrès's failure to meet at the Botanical Gardens in Madrid that triggers Carlos's re-entry to France, Carlos's imaginary trip to Perpignan to warn Juan of the police crackdown in Madrid), or kept too late (Carlos's return to Spain, his meeting with Roberto, Marianne's trip to Barcelona to find him). The exactness of time in the fiction of actions is in contrast to the indistinctness of time of the film where even past, present and future can become indistinguishable.

Marianne had been given a message by Roberto to convey

to Diego to meet Roberto at 11 am in the flat of the Central Committee (he arrives late). After the deposit of the explosives at the Gare du Lyon, Diego asks Marianne to stop at a café so he can make a phone call that he has her believe relates to his appointment with Roberto (Diego makes her believe it). At the bar, he telephones Nadine (as Domingo) to set an appointment for the next morning with her at 9 am in order to meet with her friends about their political positions and the explosives. It is that meeting that causes him to arrive late at the Central Committee. (At an earlier meeting of the Central Committee Diego is accused of having false positions as he accuses the young revolutionaries of having positions close to his own that had been condemned and that he now denies for tactical political reasons and possibly for sentimental ones relating to Nadine).

It seems as if every event or object is an opportunity for the film to initiate an itinerary which is not that of action but of associations. The suitcase with explosives is like the box of revolutionary pamphlets hidden beneath cars by Ramon and messages hidden in tubes of toothpaste, and money hidden in envelopes, and Ramon in the box of his coffin and from that to the cemetery overlooked by the flat of the young militants. It brings light, a view, they say: 'Death brings sunshine into your life' and from these exposures and uncoverings, the undressing of Marianne as he had begun to undress Nadine, to reveal a secret, awaken a passion, cover a deceit and infidelity, all of which taken together excites a desire at once true and false. And there is Nadine spreading her legs in a perfect geometric triangle, at once pure desire and pure form. In these meanderings and similitudes of objects, sites, pasts, presents, truths, deceits, Spain 1936, Spain 1962, eroticism, revolution, betrayal, the film moves not exactly forward (though it has a forward motion) but by returns, unexpected encounters, inversions, likenesses, repetitions, mirrorings, circlings.

It is by these realities of the film that its fiction is both constructed and disassembled. The fiction is not denied, only given alternative faces, other than it is and yet crucial for its existence.

When Marianne and Diego reach home after his phone call to Nadine, Diego wanders towards an embankment over the river Seine where he pauses as the camera had paused in the opening sequence at the river between France and Spain. He proposes to Marianne that they go to Spain together, not as a clandestine revolutionary but as himself, Diego Mora, and there would be no more lies and they would live a normal life.

   La Guerre est finie is a film that takes place in an instant in an interval between two rivers, two crossings, and two lives.

The next morning, overjoyed at returning to Spain (his most passionate love), Diego is met by a driver to take him to Barcelona to warn Juan. His new name is Gabriel Chauvin (*chauvinist*). The day after, sent by the Central Committee, Marianne takes a plane to warn him that he may be in danger and should not go on to Madrid. The password is 'The sun rises over Benidorm'.

   It echoes unmistakably with 'Death brings sunshine into your life'

   Buen viaje.

Alain Resnais (2)

Souvent, dans une découpage, je pars d'une image autour de laquelle se développe un mouvement d'autres images qui doivent être solidaires de la première comme le sont les éléments d'une musicale. **(Alain Resnais)**[12]

The frequent images of projections in *La Guerre est finie* are like mirages that other images give rise to. For example, during the first telephone call Carlos has with Nadine from the office of the police at the border crossing, both of them play out imaginary roles in part forced upon them (for safety) by the police presence and by the fact that it was the police who initiated the call, and in part for the delight of the play, a flirtation and a flirtation with danger.

Carlos plays at being René Sallanches, Nadine's father, and Nadine plays at being his daughter. They arrange, somewhat for the benefit of the police, and somewhat because they are intrigued, a meeting that evening. He affectionately calls her 'Chéri' on the telephone. (Later, she tells him teasingly that her father would never call her 'Chéri', but rather 'Nana' – a name at once erotic and literary – while he calls himself 'Domingo'). They are phantoms: 'Je m'appelle Nana.' 'Moi, Dimanche.' As Nana and Domingo, they make love.

12 Often, in a *découpage*, I proceed from an image around which a movement develops out of other images that must be linked to the first like elements in a piece of music.

They are not ever not themselves nor ever quite themselves either.

After the phone call, a series of images is projected of what Nadine might look like and the situations in which Carlos might find her: at a café, walking, carrying books, coming home. Each of the images are of different women. All the images are erotic and enticing in part because the women they call up are imaginary, unknown, absent and the projection is intensely private like so much else in the film (boxes, envelopes, compartments, secrets, deceits), and in part their eroticism is given to them because Carlos is not only a revolutionary. Nadine is a pure suggestion, and like most images, phantasmagoric.

The present has no unity or solidity in the film because it is the source of projections and mirages, thus images (all images are in a present tense) lose their distinctness and a fixed temporality. When, just after the border crossing sequence, Carlos meets Marie, the wife of the bookseller, she is framed twice in close-up (shining eyes, luscious lips, rapt attention) as Carlos describes to her what had happened and what his situation is. Marie becomes in the way in which she is framed, how she looks, how Carlos looks at her and how her husband regards both of them, not exactly Nadine (nor Marianne), but like them desirable, at once present (the wife of the bookseller) and imaginary (a lover of Carlos).

As the latter she is associated in other streams, other places. She reappears as a projected image when Carlos is left alone in Marianne's flat but seen from the back and in shadow 'like' the way Marianne is seen and whose erotic promise Carlos is waiting for and also like the women he sees in his first projections of Nadine whom he has just left, from the back and thereby all the more inviting.

Marie was never anything other than an image for Carlos and for the film, even when the two met for the first time. And, given the different series of unrealities in which women in the film circulate and the fact that many of the images of the revolutionaries are equally projected and unreal, this shadowy atmosphere of images affects everything, certainly any supposed stable present. The real is always something subject to projections, an image, not an objective entity. The idea of it as something outside the film which the film then represents is absurd. There is no 'before' to this film in the sense of a prior reality and thus the film is not, in the usual sense, representational.

Later, when Carlos is on the train back to Paris (to see Nadine, to see Marianne, to contact his comrades), his attention is taken by a young girl seated at a table across from him and across the aisle in the dining car. She is like the projection by Carlos imposed upon Marie when he is with her (but made absent into an image), and the inversion of actually projected images of figures (absences that are made to appear as if they are present but are purely imaginary, one of the strategies and hypnotic fascinations of both *L'Année dernière à Marienbad* and *Hiroshima mon amour*).

Distinctions of real and imaginary, present and absent, past and present, are not secure because the images of the film are not secure, even Spain is a chimera (or especially so), dreamt in France by the Central Committee (the General Strike), by the young militants (an 'objective' revolutionary situation), by Nadine (romanticism), by Marianne (responsibility), and by Carlos (comrades, affections, the past). These images coalesce with others that give them contrary and unforeseen senses, at once strengthening them and dissipating them (different Spains, different presents, different pasts, different realities). They spread out like apparitions.

Just as Carlos says one thing and that one thing is other things, and just as he is in one place and that one place is other places and, just as he is not only Carlos, the revolutionary, but also Diego and Domingo, the lover, no image in the film is what it is or rather it is that, and other things besides, hence the effect in the film of constant dispersion and dissemination.

Resnais's montage is not an operation of finding accords in relation to a succession, a logic or a continuity, but of the opening out of images towards others that they seem to call to or beckon, not exactly a link, nor a binding, but affinities.

Étienne-Jules Marey

... le corps est ici et il est là, mais il ne va pas d'ici à là ...
(**Maurice Merleau-Ponty**)[13]

The celluloid film strip is composed of individual frames with an interval between them. The film camera does not photograph continuous action but divides action into these frame fragments. The interval between frames is an interval of time effaced during projection. At the level of frame to frame, the fact of the persistence of vision covers the gap in time between frames since the first image remains imprinted on the retina during the time it takes for the successive one to appear and thus what is discontinous in filming and projection is made continuous by perception. At the level of shot to shot (each shot is made up of 24 frames that pass through the gate of the projector in one second) a change in scale or point of view can be covered (and most often is) by a dramatic, psychological and linear logic. Thus, in the breakdown of a master shot of a scene into shots that are fragments of it (details of objects, persons, action, spaces, moments), the logical and dramatic relation between shots is such as to make the break between them unremarkable. The spectator is, one might say, sutured into the continuity

13 ... the body is here and it is there, but it does not *move* from here to there.

of action represented in the shots – clearly the case in a shot counter-shot arrangement, usually of an exchange between characters. The effacement of the break is achieved in part by the maintenance of eye-line matches between shots and by the sheath of dialogue (sense) that overlays the images.

One of the perennial debates concerning film involves the difference (and opposition) between the realistic (natural, real-seeming) and the real. It goes to the heart of the mechanisms of film. For example, in the succession of shot to shot and the fragmentation it involves of larger units of space and time, the continuity achieved by the joining of these morsels, while seemingly natural (they make sense), is in fact an illusion since a wholeness in reality has been ruptured for the sake of a fictional construction. This was a position taken by André Bazin. In effect, Bazin wanted to reduce the gap between shot and shot ideally to nothing and thereby of shot and reality, so that joins would not be needed and the real fully established in its integrity rather than effaced for the sake of the consistency of the real-seeming of an illusion.

In the classical system of editing (that Bazin opposed), it was not only the real that was made inconspicuous, but so too the author. Since the realistic achieved its effects seamlessly as if unconstructed and naturally occurring, there was no need to posit an author. The events and actions that were represented effectively repressed the means that had established them as if action flowed one to the other without requiring an authorial intervention.

Paradoxically, the closer it seemed that one arrived at the real and away from the merely natural, the more present the author became. The break with the classical system gave birth to the author in the present and also retrospectively; quite simply, it revived the authors of the classics (for example, the skill of Hawks) by attending to the forms of classical construction, making them visible against the invisibility that had been their feature. A style characterised by the seeming effacement of its writing (*écriture*) was transformed by the privileging of that style, and so radically that its forms came to the surface and became its true content. Bazin's trouble with the writing of classical construction was not with its false absence but with its excessiveness.

*

Muybridge's locomotion studies were composed of fixed instances within a continuous movement. A series of different cameras were set out along a path, like a track, to take a picture of a movement at set intervals tripped by wires as a subject moved along. Each instant of a particular movement, say of a horse at gallop, a nude walking, an athlete leaping, was frozen in time in a single image, an instant in time. The images were arranged in sequence and could be read or seen as a continuum. Each image was a unity (one time, one space) and because Muybridge was concerned with delineating the background of the action, the image conformed to a traditional perspective view. It gave an effect of three dimensions just as the sequential series of images made up of instantaneities produced an illusion of movement. The time between one image and the next was effaced by the narrative of a movement in sequence.

When Marey was presented with Muybridge's studies of a bird in flight, he was disappointed. The fluttering of the wings of a bird is very rapid. In Muybridge's photographs, which were, like his other experiments, taken by multiple cameras, the images of the bird lacked precision or clarity. Moreover, given the extreme rapidity of the movement of the bird's wing, the interval between one photograph and the next, one position in time and another, was too great for Marey. Muybridge was essentially interested in *representing* action over time, Marey in the *analysis* of action over time, its decomposition into its constituents. For him, the gaps between photographs in Muybridge's work were as crucial if not more so than what was represented. Marey wanted a more complete, more detailed representation, wanted to reveal what was hidden in the gaps.

Marey used a camera-gun, that is, a single camera that followed the path of a bird in flight, taking pictures of it at very brief intervals. The result was a single image with the multiple positions of the bird, each stage or plane superimposed on the other, to appear as if it was the flight of many birds, not the multiple positions of a single one. The result was to close the gap and produce an image that included the full duration of the flight and all the positions assumed by the bird in it and not simply discrete instances of either action or time. Muybridge produced multiple photographs set out in a series of individual moments, Marey a single photograph of multiple moments.

In order to further arrive at a complete image of movement in time, Marey sought to eliminate the subject itself by finding a method that translated movement into graphic patterns by means of an inscriptor (like the trace of heartbeats in an electrocardiogram) or to eliminate the visibility of the subject by dressing it in black against a black background and affixing to its limbs markers in white cloth or paper strips or dots that would reproduce as squiggly graphic lines of movement, literally a photograph or writing of time: *chronophotographie*.

Marey was a Positivist scientist interested in quantity and measurement. He wanted to break up movement into its components and take them out of the flow of time in order to fix them into points in space and thus analyse them. His photographs, however (multiple movements in a single image), give an image where time and space overlap and interpenetrate and where nothing is solid or substantive. And to achieve the analytical precision he wanted, Marey eliminated the usual and customary dimensions of the image: its linear one-point depth perspective, its tonal modelling, the volume of its figures, its hierarchy of detail and its implied chronology (Muybridge's sequences). The single image of multiple movements is an image where time is grasped in a simultaneity not in a linearity or continuity. The search for the ideal Positivist measurable real brought Marey to positions of relativity (the interpenetration of time and space, their superimposition, the occupation by multiple objects and overlapping lines in a single space, the relativity of observation and hence of subjectivity) that is, to the very contrary of what he had sought.

Bazin had wanted to radically open the cinema to the real, a cinema that could encompass the mystery (ambiguity) and fullness of reality, and not one preconstructed, reconstructed, interpreted, centred and singularised that he associated with montage. Reality, however, is subject to time, not only its unending passing, but the multiplicities it creates in memory, imagination, and by means of compression, condensation, telescoping and overlap. Time moves along in multiple planes and the reality it creates is of differences between planes, perspectives and positions. In a film by Resnais, for example, imaginary time, real time, remembered time are set side by side such that notions of past, present, future or of real and imaginary have little or no sense. The ambiguity that Bazin valued as inherent in the real can only be found and revealed (as he recognised) by the artifices of the cinema, whether these are of shot-sequences (as in Resnais) or meticulously edited and disparate ones (also as in Resnais) is beside the point.

Bibliography

Amengual, Barthélemy 'Cinéma et écriture' in Dominique
    Noguez ed *Cinéma: théorie, lectures* Paris: Klincksieck 1973
——, *Le Cuirassé Potemkine* Paris: Nathan 1992
——, 'Renoir, Chaplin, Stroheim, Griffith' in *Du réalisme
    au cinéma* Paris: Nathan 1997 (originally in *Nouvelles
    approches de l'oeuvre de Jean Renoir*, Montpellier: Univer-
    sité Paul Valéry 1995, pp 23–37]
——, 'D.W. Griffith: le temps, l'espace, la volupté' *Du réalisme
    au cinéma* Paris: Nathan 1997
Amiel, Vincent *Esthétique du montage* Paris: Nathan 2001
Aumont, Jacques Jean-Louis Comolli, Jean Narboni and Sylvie
    Pierre 'Entretien avec Jacques Rivette. Le temps déborde'
    Cahiers du cinéma n204 septembre 1968 in Antoine de
    Baecque ed *La Nouvelle Vague* Paris: Cahiers du cinéma
    1999
——, and Michel Marie *L'Analyse des films* Paris: Nathan
    1998
——, *Les théories des cinéastes* Paris: Nathan 2002
——, *Montage Eisenstein* Paris: Images Modernes 2005
de Baecque, Antoine and Thierry Jousse *Le retour du cinéma*
    Paris: Hachette 1996
Barthes, Roland 'The Third Meaning' in *The Responsibility of
    Forms* New York: Hill and Wang 1985
Bazin, André *Qu'est-ce que le cinéma?* Paris: Les Éditions du
    Cerf 1994

——, *Jean Renoir* New York: Delta 1974

Becker, Jacques, Jacques Rivette, François Truffaut 'Le cinéma selon Howard Hawks': entretien avec Howard Hawks *Cahiers du cinéma* n56 février 1956

Benayoun, Robert, Michel Ciment, Jean-Louis Pays "Ne pas faire un film sur l'Espagne' entretien avec Alain Resnais' [*Positif* n79 novembre 1966] in Stéphane Goudet *Alain Resnais* Paris: Gallimard 2002

Bertin, Célia *Jean Renoir, cinéaste* Paris: Gallimard 1994

Bonitzer, Pascal 'It's Only a Film/où La Face du Néant' *Framework* n14 1981

——, *Peinture et cinéma: Décadrages* Paris: Éditions de l'Étoile 1995

——, *Le champ aveugle* Paris: Cahiers du cinéma 1999

Bordwell, David *The Cinema of Eisenstein* Cambridge: Harvard University Press 1993

Brenez, Nicole 'Forms 1960–2004: 'For It Is the Critical Faculty That Invents Fresh Forms' (Oscar Wilde)' in Michael Temple and Michael Witt *The French Cinema Book* London: BFI Publishing 2004

Braun, Eva *Picturing Time: The Work of Étienne-Jules Marey (1830–1904)* Chicago: University of Chicago Press 1992

Chabrol, Claude 'Entretien avec Alfred Hitchcock par Claude Chabrol et François Truffaut [1955] suivi d'un Nouvel entretien par Jean Domarchi et Jean Douchet [1959] ' in Serge Daney ed *La politique des auteurs: Les entretiens* Paris: Cahiers du cinéma 2001

Curchod, Olivier *La Grande illusion* Paris: Nathan 1994

Daney, Serge '*Vertigo*' *Ciné journal* vII/1983–1986 Paris: Cahiers du cinéma 1998 [27 mars 1984]

——, 'Resnais et l'"écriture du désastre"' [21 avril 1984] in *Ciné journal* vII/1983–1986 Paris: Cahiers du cinéma 1998

——, 'L'amour par terre' [17 octobre 1984] *Ciné journal* vII/1983–1986 Paris: Cahiers du cinéma 1998

Devaux, Frédérique L'Homme à la caméra *de Dziga Vertov* Bruxelles: Edition Yellow Now 1990

De Vincenti, Giorgio *Jean Renoir* Marsilio: Venezia 1996

Douchet, Jean *Hitchcock* Paris: Cahiers du cinéma 1999

Duras, Marguerite *Hiroshima mon amour* Paris: Gallimard 1994

Eisenstein, Sergei *S. M. Eisenstein* vI Writings 1922–34 Richard Taylor ed London: BFI 1988

Eisenstein, Sergei 'Dickens, Griffith and Ourselves' (1942) *S.M. Eisenstein: Selected Works* vIII Richard Taylor ed London: BFI 1996

Esquenazi, Jean-Pierre ed *Vertov: L'invention du réel!* Paris: Harmattan 1997

Frappat, Hélène *Jacques Rivette, Secret compris* Paris: Cahiers du cinéma 2001

Frizot, Michel *La Chronophotographie* Dijon: Association des Amis de Marey et Ministère de la Culture 1984

Fuller, Samuel *A Third Face* New York: Applause Theatre and Cinema Books 2004

Gili, Jean A *Cinéma Aujourd'hui 69: Howard Hawks* Paris: Éditions Seghers 1971

Goudet, Stéphane *Alain Resnais* Paris: Gallimard 2002

Gunning, Tom *D W Griffith and the Origins of American Narrative Film: The Early Years at Biograph* Chicago: University of Illinois Press 1994

Hillier, Jim and Peter Wollen eds *Howard Hawks, American Artist* London: BFI Publishing 1996

Ishaghpour, Youssef *Orson Welles Cinéaste: Une Caméra Visible* 3 vol Paris: Éditions de la Différence 2001

Labarthe, André S and Jacques Rivette 'Entretien avec Resnais et Robbe-Grillet' *Cahiers du cinéma* n123 september 1961

Leperchey, Sarah *Alain Resnais: une lecture topologique* Paris: Harmattan 2000

McBride, Joseph ed *Focus on Howard Hawks* Englewood Cliffs, NJ: Prentice Hall 1972

Magny, Joël *Le Point de vue* Paris: Cahiers du cinéma 2001

Mancini, Michele and Giuseppe Perella eds *Pier Paolo Pasolini: corpi e luoghi* Rome: Theorema edizioni 1981

Marey, Étienne-Jules *Le mouvement* (1894) Nîmes: Éditions Jacqueline Chambon 1994

Marie, Michel **Muriel** *d'Alain Resnais* Paris: Atlande 2005

Mitry, Jean 'Jean Renoir' in Jean Mitry *Histoire du cinéma:*

Art et Industrie vIV *les années 30* Paris: Jean-Pierre Delarge 1980

——, *Esthétique et psychologie du cinéma* Paris: Éditions du Cerf 2001

Mottet, Jean ed *Griffith* Paris: Ramsay Poche Cinéma 1984

Moullet, Luc 'Sam Fuller: sur les brisées de Marlowe' in Antoine de Baecque ed. *Le goût de l'Amérique* Paris: Cahiers du cinéma 2001 [From *Cahiers du cinéma* n93 march 1959]

Musée Marey *La passion du mouvement au XIXᵉ siècle: hommage à E J Marey* Beaune: Musée Marey 1991

Pasolini, Pier Paolo *Empirismo eretico* Rome: Garzanti 1972

Pinel, Vincent *Montage* Paris: Cahiers du Cinéma 2001

Renoir, Jean *The Rules of the Game* London: Lorimer 1970

——, *My Life and My Films* New York: Da Capo Press 1991

Riepeyrout, Jean-Louis *La Grande Aventure du Western: Du Far West à Hollywood (1894–1963)* Paris: Les Éditions du Cerf 1964

Rivette, Jacques et François Truffaut 'Entretien avec Jean Renoir' in Serge Daney ed *La politique des auteurs: Les entretiens* Paris: Cahiers du cinéma 2001

——, 'Génie de Howard Hawks' *Cahiers du cinéma* n23 may 1953

Robbe-Grillet, Alain *L'Année dernière à Marienbad* Paris: Les Éditions de Minuit 1961

Rohmer, Éric 'Alfred Hitchcock's *Vertigo*' *The Taste for Beauty* Cambridge: Cambridge University Press 1989 ['L'Hélice et l'idée'] *Cahiers du cinéma* n93 mars 1959

——, *Six contes moraux* Paris: Cahiers du cinéma 1998

Siety, Emmanuel *Le Plan* Paris: Cahiers du cinéma 2001

Table ronde sur *Hiroshima mon amour* d'Alain Resnais *Cahiers du cinéma* n97 juillet 1959 in Antoine de Baecque ed *La Nouvelle Vague* Paris: Cahiers du cinéma 1999

Taylor, Richard and Ian Christie eds *The Film Factory: Russia and Soviet Cinema in Documents 1896–1939* London: Routledge 1988

Thomas, François *L'Atelier d'Alain Resnais* Paris: Flammarion 1989

Truffaut, François *The Films in My Life* New York: Da Capo
    Press 1994
Tsivian, Yuri *Ivan the Terrible* London: BFI Publishing
    2002
Ungaro, Jean *André Bazin: généalogies d'une théorie* Paris:
    L'Harmattan 2000
Wagner, Jean 'Howard Hawks' in Raymond Bellour ed *Le
    Western* Paris: Gallimard 1994
Wood, Robin *Howard Hawks* London: Secker & Warburg:
    1968

Index

Note: 'n' after a page reference indicates the number of a note on that page